ROUSSEAU
On Education

ROUSSEAU

Edited by Leslie F. Claydon

Educational Thinkers Series

ROUSSEAU
On Education

Edited, with an Introduction, by
LESLIE F. CLAYDON

Collier-Macmillan Limited, London
THE MACMILLAN COMPANY

Collier-Macmillan Limited
10 South Audley Street, London W1

The Macmillan Company,
Collier-Macmillan Canada Ltd, Toronto

Library of Congress Catalogue Card Number: 67-17498

First printing 1969

Set in 10 on 11½ Times Linotype
Printed in Great Britain
by Richard Clay (The Chaucer Press), Ltd.,
Bungay, Suffolk

CONTENTS

NOTE ON TEXTS AND EXTRACTS

The versions of the original text of the works considered in this book are readily available to any student wishing to read Rousseau in the French. No judgment is made upon the relative merits of these versions in comparison with others.

The translation into English of the full text of *Émile ou de l'éducation* which was found invaluable as a reference in the production of this book was the translation by Barbara Foxley in the Everyman's Library Series. For *Du Contrat Social* Charles Frankel's translation in the series The Hafner Library of Classics is similarly recommended.

There is an extensive literature both about Rousseau the man and Rousseau the writer, and the bibliography lists a selection of references which were found to be of great value.

The present readings are plainly not continuous and indication of selection and discontinuity has been given by breaking the passages one from another where desirable.

REFERENCING

Wherever appropriate, references have been given to a text in French and to one in English translation. The references follow the extracts which are here translated.

E.g. (I) 30 (V) 42 following an extract refer the reader to (I) and (V) and to pages 30 and 42 respectively, where (I) and (V) indicate items in the Bibliography.

Introduction

THE MAN AND HIS WORK

Jean-Jacques Rousseau was born in the city of Geneva. During his lifetime he was to accomplish many things, but he is chiefly remembered for his writings; which range over a very wide field indeed, including music, politics and education. There is a certain unity throughout this work, however, as this Introduction will try to show.

One of Rousseau's books is entitled *Émile ou de l'éducation*. Although its fame is as an educational treatise, it was much concerned with the condition of society as he found it, particularly in France, where he lived for many years. His own city of Geneva and his adopted country, France, banished him for this work and for his political treatise called *Du Contrat Social*.

When he was a fugitive from his native city and from France, Rousseau found sanctuary with the British philosopher David Hume, who was a gentle and compassionate man. Rousseau had written of the need for fellow feeling and trust among men, yet he became pathologically suspicious of the intentions of his protector in the face of all evidence.

Rousseau wrote of the vital importance of domestic harmony and accord between man and wife; he himself was involved in a series of entanglements and illegitimate attachments. He had stated unequivocably that a child needed the care of both parents: his own children were denied the care of either by being placed in foundling homes.

In *Émile* the tutor remains with his charge over his whole education: Rousseau's career as tutor was but a year long.

Public recognition of Rousseau's abilities as a writer was first gained with an essay contending that the arts and sciences of man were a corrupting influence: Rousseau had earlier sought to take Paris by storm with a new system of musical notation. He also wrote a book on chemistry. There seems to be no end to the train of contradictions which drags across the life and work of this extraordinary man.

It is generally proper to assess the merit of what a man writes quite independently of any assessment of the man himself. In the case of Rousseau, however, there is such an intimacy of connection between the man as man and the man as writer that this is difficult at best. He wrote from himself and of himself, perfectly aware of the fact that this was so. It is not, therefore, merely a matter of supplying background information or of affording his work a context in terms of literary style which makes some account of Rousseau's life a desirable preliminary to a consideration of his writings.

No one piece of Rousseau's work stands in isolation from the rest. This is a consequence of the involvement of the man which is described above. *Émile* is not an autonomous disquisition upon the educational proprieties, a brilliant rag-bag of methodological hints and tips, nor yet only a new attack upon an old problem. It is part of a much larger project; a component of a root and branch reappraisal of the condition of civilised man which concludes with a radical proposal to reshape everything according to a totally new ground plan. Unless this is realised, one obtains a very restricted view of the book; one narrowly confined to the undoubted insights of a psychological character which it contains. Rousseau's consideration of what is to be learned and what not is disastrously ignored or misinterpreted. The central purpose of the book is missed.

Rousseau was born on June 28th, 1712. His mother died on July 7th of that year and he was given into the care of an aunt. His father was a watchmaker; a turbulent character who was twice in trouble with the Genevan authorities and who, after the second occasion, was forced to leave the place. The family was thus disintegrated when Jean-Jacques was ten years of age.

An uncle placed him in the care of a pastor in a village called Bossey, where he remained for some two years before he was attached to the office of a notary in order to acquire a means of earning a living. The placement was unsuccessful. In 1725 Rousseau was apprenticed to an engraver, but proved to be no more fitted for this occupation than for the first.

The vagrant youth received only the most unsettled and fragmentary formal schooling, but before he left the care of his father he had acquired a passion for literature and, by his own account, had read a quite astonishing amount. The love of books remained with him. While apprenticed to the engraver he sold his shirts so that he could borrow books from a library. This, coupled with companionship with adults, stands in place of a formal education for Rousseau.

A childhood absorption in romantic literature may well have fostered in the young man a sense of wonder which remained unsatisfied by a creed meagre in grandeur and magnificence such as Genevan Calvinism. At the same time he seemed to find no romance in the immediately utilitarian. He dreamed; his imagination building upon his reading unconstrained by any study which might have led him to distinguish fantasy from disciplined thought.

Striving to transcend the humdrum, he may have found certain attractions in Roman Catholicism's richness. Certainly but for an interest in Catholicism Rousseau might never have encountered the woman who perhaps did more than any other to turn him upon the paths which eventually made him celebrated. After a conversation a priest of the Catholic faith gave him a recommendation to a collecting house for would-be converts which was situated at Annécy and was run by a Mme de Warens, herself a convert. Rousseau was admitted there on Palm Sunday of 1728. Before he left again Mme de Warens had become his protector, mistress and his tormentor. Upon his arrival she was twenty-nine years of age, divorced and something of a collector of unusual and talented young men. He was seventeen.

Mme de Warens made an immediate impression upon him. She appeared to him at that time as a woman of intelligence and knowledge of the world, vitally interested in matters of great moment and tremendously assured. The young man adrift accorded her the authority over him normally granted as the due of a wise and loving mother.

They discussed many things, including religion, literature and music. Rousseau soon conceived the notion that his true métier *was* music, and it was therefore arranged that he should study under a teacher named Lemaistre. For six months he did so. Remarkably, this proved a sufficient basis for Rousseau to offer himself in the future as a teacher of music. Still later he composed an opera which was accepted for production. He came first to Paris, con-

vinced that he was to become famous as the creator of a new
system of musical notation.

For over a decade Rousseau returned again and again to 'Maman'.
He took a number of posts of one kind and another over this
period, but always arrived back at the home of Mme de Warens.
He was baptised a Catholic and stayed for a while at a Catholic
Hospice in Turin. He took service as a lackey and was taught
Latin by the master he served. Mme de Warens sent him to a
seminary, but he was back with her within two months.

This is the pattern of the relationship over the ten years, although
the nature of the relationship changed. Rousseau became 'Maman's'
lover in 1753. (He declared later that he felt as if he was committing
incest.) This apart, the story can be continued in much the same
way until 1742, when the tangled amours of Madame de Warens
and of Rousseau himself created a situation of particular difficulty
even in this curious history. During these years Rousseau learned
much which was essential to the progress he was to make. It was
yet to be a long time before Rousseau felt himself to be beyond
and above this extraordinary woman and her influence.

In 1758 Mme de Warens obtained a post for Rousseau as tutor
to the family of Jean Bonnet de Mably. His opinion of his efficiency
in this capacity is contained in *Émile*, but his first writings about
what a good education consists in are not. They are to be found
in the fragments of a memoir which Rousseau composed after this
brief year's experience.

To anyone familiar with the central theme of *Émile* the content
of this memoir is quite astonishing at first reading. It argues that
one should induct the child into society and all its petty tasks and
pleasures at the earliest possible moment. This is to save him
from the agonies of the grand passions and the cruel melancholy
that they bring. To be equipped with the tittle-tattle of fashionable
society keeps one calm, occupied and devoid of illusions and
delusions. One is too engaged to be other than happy, too busy to
be submerged (as Rousseau himself) in sadness. Nothing could be
more foreign to what is urged in *Émile*.

How can this be accounted for? The answer is to be sought in
Rousseau's own progress. Through all his history of wandering and
returning, venture, success and failure, there runs an undertone of
awkwardness as well as aspiration. The awkwardness is painfully
realised as new friends, acquaintances and patrons come his way.
The aspiration is eagerly pursued as such contacts accrue. The
one-time engraver's apprentice has schemed, blundered and loved

his way into the great houses of France. He has become skilled in music, learned Latin, debated with men of talent. He has enjoyed the affection of well-born women. Yet he remains vulnerable, uneasily conscious of himself as something of an outsider.

In the memoir he wishes for the child just what, at this stage in his life, he desires for himself. He prescribes for the tutor precisely the attributes of assurance and competence in the social arts he sees as the enviable possession of his own teachers and providers, bemoaning by contrast his own broodings and misgivings in isolation and exclusion. Insecurity and stress accompany what it is to live by unschooled wits and an undisciplined intelligence. He advocates for the child a condition of polished 'togetherness' protecting him from this constant unease.

It is plain that some sort of volte-face must occur after this time if *Émile* is to be possible. To explain its occurrence it is necessary to trace Rousseau's career through another phase: that from the time he left Mme de Warens for good and abandoned reliance upon her support.

He did not quit her company in storm and animosity for all the troubled history of the relationship. Precisely the reverse: convinced of his musical understanding, Rousseau obtained funds, by selling his books and entreating friends, so that he could return to Paris. He was convinced that he could restore his patroness's now drastically reduced funds by publishing his new system of musical notation. He therefore presented the work before the Académie des Sciences, who were conspicuously unimpressed. Defiantly he then had the system published in January 1743, but again neither fame nor fortune accrued to him. However, the appearance of the work did serve to bring him to the notice of certain well-established musical authorities of the period and then of an increasing number of people in fashionable and influential positions. He gained favour in this company.

In June 1743 he was offered a post as secretary to the ambassador in Venice. So far had he ascended the social ladder by this time that he accepted the post only upon a second invitation to do so. Yet his fate in this post was no more successful and little longer lived than in his first apprenticeship. By August 1744 he was on his way back to Paris, having been dismissed from his post for insolence. For his part he was possessed of a sense of grievance. He had no great opinion of his superior and felt the victim of a tragic injustice, a feeling unlikely to have been shared by those who had sought the opportunity for him. What he saw as misfortune they saw as folly, and this did nothing to ameliorate his sense of grievance. His attitude towards the fashionable and powerful began to change. They afforded no guarantee of deserved success; they failed to recognise merit down on its luck.

The seed of the volte-face is in this. Symptomatic of the change is the new attachment Rousseau formed at this time, (1745), to a woman most unlike 'Maman' or any of the other women of high society with whom Rousseau had had romantic associations in the past. Thérèse Levassier was then 24 years of age. She was the daughter of an ex-employee of the Orleans mint. Just what sort of person she was is something of a puzzle, for the accounts of her conflict sufficiently to suggest anything from a bitch to an angel, but it is certain that she lacked the accomplishments of the cultured and was often an embarrassment. Yet Rousseau stayed with her for the next thirty-five years. She was the mother of his children.

Rousseau's embitterment grew with the bite of increasing poverty. He was still involved in the musical world, collaborated upon an opera and had a comedy accepted for presentation. No profit came of this. Everything went badly. Eventually a post was found for him as secretary to a wealthy family. It was something of a sinecure, for he continued to write for the theatre and pursued an interest in chemistry with sufficient industry to contemplate writing a book upon the subject. However it remains that by the end of 1747 Rousseau occupied no position of importance, and his 35 years were beginning to impress themselves upon him. A brooding sense of failure ate into his thinking. Ambition and declining hope are a bitter mixture in a man, productive of aimless antagonisms.

By 1750 Rousseau had set up home with Thérèse in a rented apartment. He had come into contact with a group of philosophers, including Didérot, who were working to produce a comprehensive survey of existing knowledge accompanied by critical comment upon what they regarded as long-established errors. They were known as the Encyclopédistes. Rousseau was invited to contribute to the section on music, a chance he took gladly, not least because it afforded him an opportunity to voice his resentment of those who had paid such scant heed to his system of notation. (He wrote a letter to Mme de Warens in which he said he now had his enemies by the short hairs.)

The scope and nature of the *Encyclopédie* was bound to bring its instigators into conflict with both civil and religious authorities. Didérot, who propagated progressively more controversial views on religion, was arrested and imprisoned in July 1749. After some months he was paroled to a place in Vincennes and allowed to receive visitors, regular among whom was Rousseau.

The walk from Paris to Vincennes was a tedious one. Rousseau made a habit of carrying something to read and stopping for a while within a forest on the way there. This was how he came to read, in an issue of the *Mercurie de France*, of the competition organised by the Academy of Dijon. A prize was to be given for the best essay upon the subject as to whether the sciences and arts of the day contributed to the betterment of or corrupted the morals of men.

By his own account Rousseau was instantly inspired as if by a vision. (Didérot claimed that he supplied the enthusiast with an idea to work on, however.) He rushed to Vincennes full of the competition and left determined to produce an essay which would be worthy of the prize. He had decided to argue that the sciences and arts were corrupting influences, a point of view which contains the germ of a later and vital contention that man's progress had been from the originally good to the corrupted thing enslaved by custom. The thesis of the essay was, in fact, that however base men might be by nature, the sciences and arts served only to further their baseness, to deepen misunderstanding and to lessen sympathy between them.

The essay gained the prize, a fact of tremendous psychological importance for Rousseau, because in it he dispraised the very activities through which he had hitherto hoped and expected to gain esteem but from which he had gained no more than a casual notice and a certain amount of patronage. The essay brought him almost immediately into the full light of public attention. Opinion was generally scandalised, to be sure, but this was unimportant; the essay was a success, in that it was accorded the closest examination. Sixty-eight articles defending the sciences and arts appeared very shortly after its publication; a very different response from the scant regard he considered had been given to his previous work in music and other fields.

Rousseau now saw himself as the solitary and heroic upholder of the right and true, a sufficient compensation for the slights and injustices he felt he had received. Assurance replaced doubt. He was the only one in step. The volte-face is complete. There would be no returning to a position such as inspired the early memoir on education.

Among the critics of the essay were many of considerable reputation, including a one-time friend of Rousseau's named Charles

Bordes. In June 1751 Bordes gave a lecture at the Academy of Lyons in which he challenged Rousseau's thesis. Rousseau published a reply. Bordes returned to the attack in an essay. He asked the question as to why it was that one found it to be the common case that vice went hand in hand with ignorance. How could this be reconciled with the argument that the increase in knowledge corrupted rather than improved man? If Rousseau was right in this, one should surely find that the less a man knew, the less he was prone to immoral conduct and wrong doing.

The challenge is a fundamental one, fatal to Rousseau's case if not conclusively countered. But even the move of countering it presents a problem. In attempting to provide information, to explain and enlighten, Rousseau could be accused of wrecking his case by relying upon an increase of knowledge to make a point that increase of knowledge is of no value!

Rousseau must thus make not one move but two to preserve his position from destruction. Firstly, he must refute the contention that is implicit in Bordes' attack, that man was originally evil or base as well as ignorant, for, if this was so, then the closer to his original state he was, the deeper in vice he would be found to be. Secondly, to permit a counter without creating a paradox, Rousseau must show that what is at fault is not the possession of knowledge as such but the manner and utilisation of knowledge gained through the study of the sciences as they were taught and made use of at the time.

To accomplish these ends Rousseau wrote *Émile*.

It was no small task, nor was it one complete in itself. If its origin can be traced to a question put in 1752, the answer it received took much time to build. Bordes' challenge was to inspire an assault upon the entire structure of society as Rousseau found it, an indictment of all that had thwarted and blunted his early aspirations. Rousseau assumes the position of an inspired corrector of the world's error. *Émile* is a major thrust in an attack intended to provide an alternative basis for society, free of the flaws afflicting the present one, which mishandled the sciences and arts to blunt and twist the searching soul of man. It would take time, and during that time, ironically enough, Rousseau was successful in a number of ventures within the domain of the arts. In the years 1752–53 he published the preface to a play (in which he attacked the sciences) and a letter unfavourably comparing French with Italian music, to both which publications there was a spate of learned objections all serving to maintain Rousseau in the public eye.

Then, in December 1753, the *Mercurie* published details of a new essay competition. This time the subject was 'What is the Origin of Inequality amongst men and is it authorised by the Natural Law?' Rousseau again set himself to compose an entry. He professed no quasi-divine intimations that he should do so, but, as he became engrossed in the work, he did become possessed by somewhat mystical pre-occupations if his testimony in *The Confessions* is to be believed. In that book he describes how he would make his way into the forests about Saint-Germain, whence he had gone to write in peace, and reflect upon the history of mankind, perceiving as in a vision the monstrous lies men have told of themselves as they trekked from the path of the natural, following a false model of perfection. It appears that he felt his spirit rise towards the divinity and to look down upon the blind meanderings of all men so misled.

From out of this experience he was able to construct the thesis of his essay. Strip man's nature naked and one discovers an innocent, but the pretended perfection of man as he has made himself at the dictate of fashion and artifice has debased him, bringing him misery, suffering and conflict. The inequalities among men do not belong to them in a state of nature; they are symptomatic of the conditions he finds himself in as a consequence of not following the natural in himself.

The essay was dedicated to Geneva. Rousseau was shortly to re-apply for Genevan citizenship and to return to the Protestant faith. To renounce his affiliation with France and with Catholicism was, perhaps, yet another way to denounce those by whom he had felt so scurvily treated. Perhaps also it was the case that his growing eminence constrained the authorities to accept him despite obvious marks of unsuitability. (He was, for example, not married to Thérèse at this time.)

Other breaks were made by Rousseau. On his way back to Geneva he visited Mme de Warens for the last time. He describes in *The Confessions* the change he saw in her, this woman he had once admired above any as brilliant and accomplished. No doubt she was changed and no doubt Rousseau did feel a certain sadness about that, but it is also a very different Rousseau. Pity can be a form of triumph. How easily might he have remained unaware that his former mistress was brilliant and accomplished only in terms of the false perfections of artifice!

Some breaks were less convenient and were not of Rousseau's instigation. Although he had had an article on political economy

published in the fifth volume of the *Encyclopédie* in 1775, a certain
long-felt distrust of him among the prime movers of the project was
rapidly spreading. A more or less complete rupture was imminent.
It was precipitated by the publication in the *Encyclopédie* of an
article upon the Genevan Republic written by one D'Alembert, who
was then staying with Voltaire near to Geneva itself. The article
was commendatory in intention but not in effect, for it regretted
the Republic's failure to permit the staging of Voltaire's theatrical
works, its ban upon any sort of theatre and, furthermore, it praised
the Genevan clergy in terms which Rousseau straightaway realised
would offend against their views of themselves and the tenets of
their teaching. Nervous lest his known association with the circle to
which D'Alembert also belonged should connect him in some way
with the article, Rousseau wrote and published in 1758 a letter
pointing out the errors in the article. The Encyclopédistes regarded
this as a hostile and disloyal act.

A footnote to the letter contained a disguised reproach to Didérot
in connection with Rousseau's unsuccessful overtures towards a
Mme d'Houdetot. None of this created any good feeling and eventually led to the expulsion of Rousseau and Thérèse from *l'Ermitage*,
a place afforded him upon his return to France from Geneva by an
intimate of the *Philosophes* named Mme d'Epinay. (The stay in
Geneva was not long lived; there was insufficient opportunity for
Rousseau there.)

The remove presented no small problem. There was little money,
and Rousseau had no liking for the idea of returning to Paris to
take up some employment. He had decided that his life's work lay
in writing and that he could do this only in the peace of the country.
The couple managed to secure something of a ruin called *Mont
Louis*, which stood near by. The study in this place lacked some
of its floorboards and part of its roof. The situation could hardly
have been to anyone's liking. Despite tentative overtures of recon-
ciliation towards his former friends, it became clear that neither
they nor their friends wished to have further contact with Rousseau,
who was now ill and worried.

However, in 1759 a musical play from Rousseau, for which he
received 40,000 badly needed francs, was performed in Paris and
won favour. The Maréchal and Maréchale du Luxembourg and a
number of influential people discovered that Rousseau was resident
in the area of their Chateau. They sought his acquaintance, discovered his circumstances and offered Rousseau an apartment while
Mont Louis was put under repair. Once again therefore Rousseau

found himself beneath the roof and under the eye of a great lady. *The Confessions* contains a quite fascinating description of the mixture of feelings he had about this situation and similar ones he had previously experienced. In relationships with women of this stamp the awkward and aspiring in him reasserts itself in the shape of a nervous desire to please and a lack of confidence that he could do so. It seems that it was always easier for Rousseau to combat the opposition of men in the context of public controversy than to face the disapproval of any woman for whom he entertained the slightest regard. The urge to defer, so marked all that time ago with Mme de Warens, reasserted itself now.

There is more than psychological interest in this. The apparent disparity between the behaviour of the man in re-entering the world of the fashionable and the condemnation of just that world in his writing may lead to our dismissal of him as a hypocrite, devoid of honesty. This would be somewhat uncharitable. Rousseau did have a quite extraordinary gift for misrepresenting himself, but the disparity cited above may show not dishonesty but failure, agonisingly experienced.

In order to maintain some status with his patroness Rousseau read her his novel *La Nouvelle Héloïse,* which not only contains a number of important clues about Rousseau's own experience of women and love but also has a plot woven upon a fabric which is in accord with the thesis of his second discourse. The Maréchale liked the novel, although it is doubtful that she saw this second facet of it.

In December 1760 the book was published in London. In January of the following year it was published in Paris. It was very well received in both places, to Rousseau's enormous gratification. He had felt that writing the novel had been something of an indulgence; that it was of much less significance than the other work he was engaged upon at the time. If the novel enjoyed this success there was reason to hope that these works would receive a similar reception. *Émile* was one of these. The illusion was to be short lived.

Now the Maréchale had no great opinion of Rousseau's business ability and thought him to be suffering at the hands of the publisher he used. By her direction therefore *Émile* was placed with a different publisher than the one dealing with the second of the works Rousseau had such hopes for by now, namely *The Social Contract.* This was most unfortunate. To begin with, *Émile* was intended to lead on to the other book; secondly, the separate publishers help to strengthen a misconception that the two works are independent of each other; a misconception originally fostered by the fact that the split of publishers brought it about that *The Social Contract* was published before *Émile*.

Rousseau's work is open to criticism in many ways. Some of these criticisms will be discussed in the following section of the Introduction. However, to the extent that the historical accidents above are responsible for the idea that *Émile* is a programmatic recommendation for an existing society rather than an allegory set forth to give guiding principles for the new society of the *Social Contract*, criticism of Rousseau is unfounded. This is a crucial point for a fair assessment both of Rousseau and of the two books concerned.

The publication of both books caused a storm. By the end of May the Censor of France had instructed the police that sales of *Émile* were to be banned. In June the Sorbonne pronounced the book to be pernicious. Shortly afterwards a warrant was issued for the arrest of the author. Both works were publicly burned in Paris and Geneva. So much for the fantasy of acceptance and acclaim built upon the success of the novel.

Rousseau was once more the outcast and the heretic, fugitive from outraged public opinion. The tragedy is that, wrong as Rousseau's thesis may or may not be, it was not exposure of it to rational examination that he experienced but a bludgeoning by prejudice which quickly turned to savage personal villification. He was hounded rather than challenged. He wrote in *The Confessions* that it seemed to be that people in France and Geneva saw him as such a monster that they wondered how it was that he was allowed to breathe. As he travelled from place to place in hectic insecurity public enmity spread out from France and Geneva to The Hague and to Neuchâtel, where he was afforded protection by the Jacobite Governor, a Scot named Lord George Keith. His letters were publicly burned and his house in Neuchâtel was stoned. In September 1765, through the good offices of Lord Keith, he was received in England by David Hume, the British philosopher.

In London he was once more the eminent man to be fêted and visited and invited, but within eighteen months all this was transformed again and the visit ended in discord and animosity. Rousseau was by now showing signs of a capacity for suspicion bordering on the pathological, in that it frequently appeared to have little or no foundation in fact to warrant it. It is possible that the shock received when there was so violent a reaction against what he had hoped to be celebrated works is not unconnected with this psychological deterioration. At any rate, the situation worsened until it was inevitable that he and Thérèse should leave England; he was convinced (from his report in *The Confessions*) that his ill repute in that country was then such that it could not be remedied in his lifetime.

The Confessions is not merely a book of detailed reminiscence. It might have been a little less infused with suspect interpretations had it been such. Rousseau was actively engaged in a counter-attack in defence of his work and his own personal reputation, of which *Confessions* is an integral part. In it he sought to bring together his own thought and experience as an individual and the theses underpinning both *Émile* and *The Social Contract*. He wished to demonstrate that he was not, of himself, blameworthy for the sins and failings which the book revealed of himself. He, as others, was victim of the corrupting influence of a society quite different and infinitely inferior to the one he set out as possible in his writings. So long as what he proposed was not only left unimplemented but also attacked as evil or worthless, then the blameworthiness rested upon those who discounted him, not upon himself, who was victim rather than perpetrator. He was engaged in a tremendous effort to persuade.

In so far as *The Confessions* had this function, it was a failure, even though, while living in one place and another, he was invited to give readings of the work. These sponsored readings titillated the company before whom he read but caused general scandalisation and attempts to have them prevented.

Rousseau did not surrender. He produced two more major works of a similar nature, the *Dialogues* and then *Les Rêveries du Promeneur Solitaire*. In both he tried, by further lengthy and (apparently) frank examination of his own life, to show that the natural and good in man is hounded from him by one social influence or another.

The enterprise is heavily overlain by much that is irrational and even fanciful. Nevertheless, these two strange documents are worth regard, for they show a genuine concern for the individual and his desperate requirement for a social environment preservative and permissive of the emergence of the best in him. Both works are informed by the twin questions, 'What ought I to have done?' and 'Why could I not do it?': queries which are surely as relevant today as then.

Finally, Rousseau returned to Paris. He married Thérèse at last, lived by copying music and similar lowly occupations, and descended steadily into extremes of poverty and ill health. He died in 1778, at Ermonville, where he was living by the kindness of yet another patron.

There is a curious sequel. In 1794 his remains were transferred to an officially selected resting place of honour in Paris. In twenty years one epoch had ended in blood and despoliation and another had taken its place, boasting the slogan of liberty, equality and fraternity. It was soon to be despotically governed by Napoleon, who would gather most of Europe beneath the dominion of France. One may wonder what Rousseau would have made of such an outcome. He had asked himself the question as to how one could guarantee liberty and equality. He had abhorred violence. One may see in him the mark of the true revolutionary. How true the French Revolution was to Rousseau's ideas is another matter and beyond the province of this book.

The chapters which follow will be devoted principally to extracts from Rousseau's own writings. Something of their nature has already been described, but a more detailed discussion is necessary from which and to which the reader may move.

The place of *Émile ou de l'éducation* in the over-all plan of Rousseau's work has been set out in the preceding section of the Introduction. The purpose informing the book is to be discovered at its very outset. Rousseau states a basic premiss. Man is a meddler who manipulates and distorts the design of the 'author of nature' out of all recognition, pursuing this folly to the ultimate by following the same course in respect of man himself.

Example after example is provided, all purporting to embody Rousseau's own observation of this disastrous course of action. One sees immediately that they are strictly confined to that section of French society possessed of power, wealth and leisure, and this requires no further explanation than has been attempted in the first section. A contrast is continually being drawn by Rousseau between this social group or class and that of the humble folk of France, who, it is suggested, are freer of social distortions and manipulations than their 'betters'. However, Rousseau is careful not to grant them complete clearance; he freqently makes a second contrast between France of his day and the far-off societies of, say, the Caribbean Islands (distance) or the ancient civilisations (time).

The basic premiss yields two important propositions, which guide the direction of the whole work.

(a) What is thought of as wisdom is merely slavish subscription to received opinion.

(b) The granting of this subscription chains us to the interests and influences which find these opinions conservative of their power and influence.

The direction of the attack is clearly indicated; it is against the artifices of society. In *Émile* it takes the form of pointing out the enormity of educating with the intention of fostering subscription to them in the receptive and helpless child, so robbing him of innocence and denying him the possibility of achieving real wisdom. Plainly only the already corrupted could perpetrate such a thing. Rousseau now sets out to exemplify this. All the talk about right posture and the protection of the helpless babe, which is supposed to justify such practices as swaddling, becomes, by Rousseau's account, no more than an elaborate and baseless system of excuses for the abandonment of the most fundamental of duties, the most natural of functions; the care and sustenance of a baby by its own mother.

The main point of the first part of *Émile* is the substantiation of the charge. From the very outset, it is maintained, we have moved away from the 'path of nature'. Every step we take drags the child farther away from his true nature and into the ways of the corrupted things we are.

A caution is necessary here, however. We should not think that Rousseau requires a return to nature in the sense of some sort of retreat into primitivism, although his frequent references to the Caribs does nothing to help us avoid the mistake. It is rather the case that he urges that we follow the dictates of nature without jettisoning our potentialities for advance in wisdom and power.

But the recommendations stemming from the policy of proceeding 'according to nature' still possess a certain starkness, and Rousseau was nervously well aware of the fact. He goes to some pains to show that the endurance of hardship is as inevitable and beneficial to the growing child as is growth itself. He makes a number of interesting moves to persuade the reader to his view. For example, we are asked to defer not to '*the* natural' but to the guidance of a 'she', rather as the Greeks referred to this or that Goddess, to the author of a design which it is beyond the capacity of mere man to improve upon, even when hardship *is* involved.

Then, to strengthen his case further, Rousseau cites two alleged and commonly accepted facts. In the France of his time a high rate of mortality persisted among children below the age of eight years. Secondly, children who were 'delicately reared' were more likely to die than those not so carefully protected.

Now it is relatively easy to find particular examples in this way, and to neglect the fact, or blind others to it, that one can just as easily produce examples which support an opposite point of view. This is particularly true with the example just mentioned. We can turn Rousseau's own claim that many children in France died before becoming eight years of age against his argument. Were all these children medically attended? This is doubtful enough, but it is still more doubtful whether they were attended by the sort of 'fashionable' doctor who receives so much criticism from Rousseau; the part charlatan whose medical advice is tailored to what it will please the patient to hear and so bring in a large fee. It seems possible to point to many infant deaths not caused or assisted by such deadly ministrations. Rousseau's example by no means establishes the invariable beneficence of nature.

On the other hand, we can readily agree that a certain amount of hardening is important for the healthy development of the child. He must stand at risk to some extent if he is to exercise his growing powers of locomotion and so forth. That this is so does not entail acceptance of Rousseau's contentions, however. It does not follow that it is the suffering of pain as such that is beneficial. It is not shown that we must accept some pain and cruelty to escape something worse. Before this last proposition is accepted it must be demonstrated that suffering some pain does prevent later and greater cruelty and pain.

Rousseau does not show this. It is true that he does state later on and in a quite different context (a discussion of the distinction between man as himself and man as a citizen: i.e. Frenchman or Englishman) that where we are 'pulled this way by nature and that way by man' the resulting inner conflict—which constitutes the more cruel and painful—does occur, but one cannot make a direct transposition from this to the present discussion. It is not obvious that inner conflicts and emotional upheavals, caused in adult life, or even sooner for that matter, are prevented by any sort of up-bringing in infancy. Suppose a mother to heed Rousseau's strictures. She neither swaddles the infant, puts him to a nurse nor does she coddle him herself. Consequently he falls from time to time, bumps himself against objects and contracts minor ailments while building up immunity against more deadly diseases. To begin with it is somewhat fanciful to say that he suffers in the way implied by the statement, 'Suffering is the lot of man', which implies a constant background of pain. Ignoring this, however, it remains the case that it is no logical contradiction to say that such a child could grow to experience the unhappiness and anguish of acute inner conflict. Indeed, Rousseau himself says later that a great deal more than has so far been ensured is necessary if such a possibility is to be obviated.

Finally, in defence of nature, even when uncharitable or seeming to be so, Rousseau argues for a somewhat ruthless approach to the child. There is little in what he says which caters for the weak or sickly, even though he is bound to acknowledge the inconvenient truth that such children do exist. He seeks to show that no good can come of attempts to preserve that which nature has decreed shall cease. He sophisticates this argument to protect it against a charge of callousness by purporting to explain the sickly child as none of nature's doing at all. It is only because there have been generations of departure from the natural that there has been a progressive deterioration—man meddling with man has produced the sorry result. Thus the biblical saw is turned upside down to become that the transgressions against the parents shall be visited upon the children unto the third and fourth generation.

It is important to keep in view this implication of application over generations of human beings. The whole of *Émile* is written as an antidote to what has gone wrong with the human being as a species. It cannot therefore be taken in isolation, as has been explained in the previous section; the task is to correct centuries of degeneration by a radical change of direction. In this sense Rousseau is a true revolutionary; few things must remain as they are.

Having taken these steps to save his contention that experience of adversity is no argument against the recommendation to rear and educate according to nature, Rousseau later extends the claim to have relevance even to the beginnings of language in the child. The infant feels a need, perhaps to possess or handle an object some distance from him. He indicates his need by making sounds of distress that the object is not within reach. Rousseau sees this situation as involving the first stages in the acquisition of language. This is to the good, but it must be understood that the situation demands something *of* the child much more than that something be done *for* him. Once the child has been carried to distant objects which he has attempted to reach and distressed himself upon finding he cannot just stretch out a hand for them, once he has gained the ability to distinguish between the near to hand and the distant, one must be careful about continuing this practice or, alternatively, of carrying the object to the child. The child must set himself to gain the ability to reach what he desires or he must learn to tolerate his weaknesses until he can overcome them. By Rousseau's account the child cries mainly because it experiences strong feelings in respect of its own lack of power. Nothing is gained when things are done for the child to cancel out this weakness, which nature will remedy providing that man does not distort the process. In a simple society there are no servants to fetch and carry and too many things to be done for either parent to act as lackey.

Moving now to a discussion of what would today be termed the 'roles' of the mother and father, one discovers that Rousseau is not always so able to assist his case by making reference to what occurs in the simple or primitive group. We have seen that his first concern is to point to what happens now and to condemn it because it is in no way demanded by nature, and in respect of maternal duties the case is bolstered by comparison with Caribs, etc. When it comes to fathers a comparison is made here also, but we notice a change in that the Caribs or the Peruvians cannot serve. Rousseau has a footnote which refers to Plutarch's report that Cato, the Roman Censor, a man with many administrative and political cares, still contrived to bring up his sons and grandsons from their cradles.

This is a curious stratagem. It seems somewhat doubtful as to the extent to which the Roman civilisation could escape the criticisms Rousseau levels at his own. No doubt this is partly explained by Rousseau's somewhat idealistic picture of both Ancient Rome and Greece, gained at his father's knee, but one may also entertain a suspicion that any stick will do to beat the dog of his own contemporary society.

A second difference where fathers are concerned is that the hireling tutor, engaged to relieve the father of the duties Cato apparently did not shirk, is not said to usurp the father's place. It appears that the child loses a father and teacher and gains no more than a flunkey who teaches. This is not quite the same result as is supposed by Rousseau in respect of the mother substitute. The nurse may oust the mother from her place in the child's affections as well as perform the functions properly hers alone.

Combing the consideration of the roles of both parents Rousseau produces a hypothesis of considerable interest. To begin with the fate of the family structure is seen as determined by the attitudes and behaviour of the mother. Secondly, there is a modern sociological flavour to the whole discussion. A 'culture pattern' is presented to us here: the subject of the discussion is the social unit of the family as it is caught up in the larger patterns of the society. The individual mother or father is once more shown to be trapped and snared by the customs and fashions of this larger group. The underlying intent of *Émile* is constantly in view. Man is trapped by his society. He can do nothing.

At this point Rousseau lands himself in something of a dilemma. From his lonely vantage point he points still to the prevailing condition of society and declares again his contempt for it and for those who have permitted themselves to become enmeshed in it. He will have no part of it, for then he would be as they are, unable to do what should be done and incapable of rectifying the state of affairs which has brought them to their plight.

But if it is the case that there is a certain inevitability about the pattern of family life within the section of society which is the main target of his attack, as seems to be suggested by the sketching out of what we would now call a culture pattern, then there is also something odd about the indictment of the individual who is victim of it. It is strange to condemn the individual for the fault which is not of his making and which is not to be avoided. Yet this seems to be what is happening. We can recall the account of infancy and the way in which the tiny child is inducted into wilfulness and obstinacy before he is capable of resisting the pressures which so corrupt his nature.

Let us concede this but remember that Rousseau, throughout his life and work, found himself in the position of seeking to persuade to his way of thought those very people whom his thesis principally condemned. Now whether the prosecutor is in the right or in the wrong, it is rarely the case that anything approaching universal acclaim is accorded from those who find themselves so assailed. The modern sociologist will tell us that the group is a conservative agency, and he may provide us with techniques of persuasion and personnel management which soften the blow when the point is put, techniques which leave the recipient grateful for help rather than aware of blameworthiness. Rousseau, it could be said, chose his own weapons rather than selecting palliatives offered by others. His task was consequently the more difficult.

Chief among his weapons was rhetoric. Now it is frequently and properly pointed out that Rousseau is guilty of inconsistency time and again, but it must be borne in mind that sometimes what is identified is really a tactical manoeuvre. The individual man, Rousseau knew as well as does the modern sociologist, tends to dismiss

unpalatable comment when there is a chance to see what is said
as being merely general comment. He finds this considerably more
difficult, if even less palatable, when, as is often the case in *Émile*,
the reference is to *a* man, to any one man who, as say a father, finds
himself in the situation described. There may indeed be a certain
injustice in Rousseau's indictment of the trapped individual, but
there is greater impact.

Of course, the situation presented to the individual remains a
bleak one, full of anxieties. Man in general can be piloted out of his
dilemma only when the particular individual has swallowed the
bitter pill of his degeneration and joined Rousseau in the resolve
that things be changed. The test of Rousseau as a revolutionary
thinker is the degree to which he achieved this *general* effect rather
than any particular effect.

Yet another problem which Rousseau must face is the obvious
query as to why, in view of all that has so far been said, propose that
there be a tutor to *Émile*. A first step to answering this is that the
nature of the work is not that of a manual of procedure. A rescue
operation is required if mankind is not to fall further into degeneration. Someone must map out the programme for it, but Rousseau's
task is to put out guide lines as to its character rather than to detail
its form.

Is a programme possible at all? The affirmative answer given by
Rousseau rests upon the claim that man has only to look for
guidance to nature to discover the sort of thing that can and must be
done. Secondly, the possibility of the project is evidenced by the fact
that some men at least (or *a* man at least) can recognise the necessity and venture upon the prior, if easier, task of alerting others to
it.

He is not yet out of the wood, however. Whatever element of
analogy there is in the idea of a tutor, Rousseau still has to deal with
his own argument that it is only when the father fails to fulfil his
role in its entirety that the provision of a tutor must be made. But
then one laments the lack. One does not turn it into a positive and
generalised proposal.

Rousseau retreats still further into the hypothetical at this point.
To point out the nature of the revolutionary plan one must pluck
a pupil from the air as it were, one without flaws either in himself
or ones which had been foisted upon him. Any child of flesh and
blood not receiving a totality of care from his own mother and
father could not be such, and any actual child receiving this care in
society as it is, must, of necessity, be corrupted. A child not spoiled

in either of these ways will thrive as the tutor follows the principles proposed: it is up to someone to devise the necessary programme from them to suit the actual child.

The expedient of creating an imaginary pupil is only a first step of course. It allows Rousseau to legislate that there be no flaws in him as he comes to the tutor. This done, the second consideration is that no flaws are inflicted upon him after birth and before the tutor receives him. Bearing in mind the proposition that the nurse is the real mother (which is why the mother should nurse), and the further one that the only proper tutor is the father, there can be only one expedient. Rousseau makes the apparently paradoxical statement that 'Émile is an orphan whether he has a mother or father or not'. This must be read as meaning that, whether the mother and father of the child are alive or not, if there is a tutor for Émile who is not his father, then Émile is to be regarded *as if* an orphan and from the very outset at that. The tutor assumes the role of father but for the duty of providing for the material well-being of the child.

Immediately one sees that the *relationship* involved is a special one and of supreme importance. Rousseau is not talking of a sort of male governess or caretaker, nor yet of an instructor or preceptor, a flunkey who teaches. For him the term 'tutor' carries very different implications. It must do if one is to be at all satisfied that he has overcome his problem.

If the child has a tutor of the calibre indicated as necessary the latter will be the source of all authority. He will oversee the nurse so that none of the malpractices which have been discussed are allowed to occur. Rousseau proposes that he will oversee her in her diet, her living conditions and in the assessment of her temperamental suitability.

The tutor is in no way a professional with a limited sphere of activity and jurisdiction bounded by details of a particular service given for payment. This would be utterly inappropriate to the comprehensive nature of Rousseau's notion of what education is. The tutor occupies a position in Rousseau's thinking similar to other figures in his political works such as 'the man of genius', the lawgiver and, in some instances, the king or ruler. All of these are men of vision, unaffected by the corrupting influences of society. They are therefore able to realise and work for the elimination of the factors possessed of this influence, hence they are granted the legislative supremacy each is invested with in the various works.

But it might be thought to be very justifiable to inquire why

Rousseau has it *this* way round. We are to educate according to nature. What more natural a thing is there, by Rousseau's own account, than the care of a mother for her own child? Why should she not direct and control the tutor?

One explanation could be that Rousseau just did not see this alternative at all, and so did not deal with it. A second could be that a nurse could not have the freedom from corruption which the tutor possesses. A third possibility is that, for Rousseau, education extends from infancy to adulthood and through all the vicissitudes of living which this time will contain, during which the tutor never leaves his charge for any other nor does he fail to oversee every aspect of the progress. The tutor is therefore a most versatile and wise person in a great many directions; more so than one could reasonably expect any mother to be, or want her to be either, because this would be unnatural for a woman. Whichever stands, it is made still plainer now that 'tutor' must not be given a narrow interpretation if Rousseau is to be understood aright.

This last point leads Rousseau to make a number of interesting distinctions. He contrasts his 'tutor' with the terms 'master' and 'teacher' and/or 'preceptor'. It seems plain that by 'master' Rousseau refers to one equipped with the understanding and knowledge of the 'science of human duty'. For any sort of intimation of the content of this science one must go beyond *Émile*, although, since Rousseau has already stated that a 'judicious though ignorant (unschooled) father' may better educate his son than the cleverest teacher in the world, we can suppose that the mastery involved here is not to do with the areas of knowledge which, when unattained in a man, yield the term 'ignorant'. We may also suppose from this that Rousseau would wish us to gather that a clever teacher is not, of necessity, a judicious man. Plainly also, the tutor *must* be judicious, and this will involve being master of the rather nebulous science of human duty. We may gather from the comment about the fitness of an unschooled father to educate that what is involved is sound judgment and conduct in life rather than concern with some particular form of thought or combination of forms of thought.

Rousseau's account correctly implies that, to be a teacher, is to engage in some activity with the intention that a pupil shall learn as a consequence. However, some things are learned but better not taught. Sound judgment and moral actions are better arrived at through the efforts, mistakes, experiments and reflections of the simple individual himself than through receiving and following the dictates of another, the teacher. What happens when this latter procedure is adopted is no more than the acquisition of conventional patterns of behaviour. One knows 'the done thing' and no more. We are thus already well on the way to enslavement by custom. Judgment is diminished to prejudice, thought is tramlined, action becomes stereotyped. All behaviour is routinised performance.

Now this is all right up to a point, but only up to a point. The mistake in the account is a serious one. The variety of activities which can fall under the category of teaching is quite illegitimately restricted to those which might make Rousseau's argument incontestable. What a teacher does is not confined to, and need not even include, 'the giving of precepts' if by this we are to mean the issuing of solemn injunctions upon the back of a deal of even more solemn sermonizing.

Explaining, examining, demonstrating, questioning and answering may all be included under the activity described as teaching, and so, too, may 'guiding' unless one legislates that the meaning to be attached to that word will exclude the other activities just given. This would be extremely difficult to uphold, of course, and Rousseau most certainly does not do so, with the result that, as one reads on in *Émile*, one finds that the tutor does teach.

There is a second confusion in the account. The tutor, it is maintained, must be a master of the 'science of human duty'. This may or may not be so. What is certainly not the case is that one who is a master of something is, of necessity, a good instructor, teacher or guide (tutor) of that something. Similarly, the teacher who is not a judicious man cannot be automatically discounted as a possible master of something. To have mastery of something is not logically tied to instructing, teaching or guiding. For example, we may call a man a master baker even when he downright refuses to have anything to do with assisting others to bake. The sole criterion is whether or not he attains to certain standards of baking in his own work. It could even be allowed that he never baked anything in the presence of another person or ever watched any other person bake. Although the 'science of human duty' is obviously different from bakery, the conceptual point still holds.

If, therefore, Rousseau is seeking to deny the possibility of mastery to the teacher, even when he *is* a giver of precepts, his argument quite fails to achieve its end. It would seem that the distinction between tutor and teacher rests upon something quite apart from considerations of mastery or of the giving or withholding of precepts. It rests upon the sort of relationship supposed between tutor

B

and pupil in comparison with that supposed between teacher and pupil. Even then the distinction must surely concern tutor and *professional* teacher. The nearest one can get to clearing up the muddle is to say that the tutor incorporates the concept of teacher and, at the same time, modifies and governs the scope of the latter concept to all but exclude that kind of teaching which is sometimes referred to today by the somewhat enigmatic term 'direct teaching'.

Now it would be true to say that the professional teacher could not and would not want to establish precisely the sort of relationship which Rousseau's tutor has with *Émile*. He is not then bound by the restriction of manner of teaching which applies to the tutor. Once we have this clear we need not take Rousseau to be saying that the tutor may not teach but only that he may not teach in certain ways. For the present day we may take from Rousseau the valuable insight that the 'role of the teacher' is inclusive of more things than the activity of teaching and that these things may exercise a considerable influence upon the manner of teaching.

This may shed some light upon the mysterious term, 'science of human duty' as it is used by Rousseau. It seems that what is meant by it has its modern equivalent in such phrases as 'understanding of human nature', 'right attitudes towards people', and 'respect for persons'. These are not without their own problems when they are used with the same lack of explication Rousseau allows for 'science of human duty'. Alternatively, it might be argued with some justice that Rousseau was anticipating the emergence of the social sciences as we know them, the contemporary concern to make disciplined study of human behaviour and to use the results to solve problems of intolerance and maladjustment, both between individuals and between groups of people. To the extent that this can be maintained, Rousseau emerges as a subscriber to the notion of education as a process of socialisation—a somewhat strange possibility for the champion of man as and for himself. Yet another alternative is to argue that what is supposed in the human individual is an innate or natural morality from which he is deviated by social pressures. Education now appears as that which should equip man to resist these pressures. It is impossible to settle the problem with any conclusiveness. All the alternatives are plausible, in that all find some support within the work, a fact that indicates the contradictions to be found in Rousseau's thesis. All that is plain is that, in Rousseau's view, the science of human duty is neither to be equated with nor attained through study of the traditional areas of knowledge as he knew them and the manner of their teaching.

Rousseau points out the folly of separating the function of the teacher from the relationship supposed between child and tutor by asking the rhetorical question whether one would wish to make a parallel distinction between 'pupil' and 'scholar' (disciple). This stratagem tells us something about what Rousseau sees as the activity and cast of mind necessary in the individual being educated. It reinforces the exclusion of precept-giving from the activity of teaching as the latter activity is practised by the tutor. In the notion of either scholar or disciple there are implications of the giving of a voluntary submission to what is requisite and of active subscription to the task in hand as possessed of intrinsic worthwhileness. The scholar addresses himself to the business of learning, of informing himself, of seeking information and knowledge for himself, rather than sitting back and waiting to be taught. The disciple is not merely or even essentially a follower, but rather he is one who upholds in himself understood principles, and of choice refers his actions to them. He is not one who is constantly told what it is proper to do and is happy to be so ruled. Nevertheless of course, both scholar and disciple may *seek* to be taught at times.

What Rousseau is asking here is whether it is possible to consider it to be sufficient to have a pupil who, being neither scholar nor disciple, lacks all this. He would not ask the question were it not that an affirmative answer is difficult to imagine. The tactic may blind us to the possibility that one is not always able to secure these attributes in an individual without having to pilot him through a condition and attitude of mind which Rousseau ascribes to 'pupil'. Rousseau, of course, counters this by contending that this should never happen; that rather than adopt this course one should do nothing and await the signs of interest, etc., which will avoid it. This is where the term 'negative education', which is applied to Rousseau's scheme, has its application. More importantly, the counter indicates the predomination of psychological criteria in Rousseau's argument which will become increasingly evident as one progresses through the book. Much of the second book of *Émile* evidences all of this. See, for example, the manner in which the child comes to measure with any accuracy (Chapter 2, page 78).

Once again Rousseau anticipates what is to come at a later time. The doctrine of interest and the importance of sense experience are central to the educational recommendations of John Dewey. Before Dewey, Pestalozzi and Froebel advanced methodologies which owed much to the thinking of Rousseau.

Now fully concerned with a discussion of *Émile* himself, the new man in the making, Rousseau has a number of things to say in the first section of the work about the fit subject for education. Who stands most in need of education, where 'education' means what Rousseau contends it should mean? The answer must be that it is the child most subject to the distortions of fashion and custom. In France one will find him in the family of the convention-ridden people of the town and the world of business and fashion.

Notice here that the basis for this selection is in no way grounded in any contention that there is an innate superiority in the child of favoured parents. Quite the opposite in fact. Unless they are rescued they are doomed. By removing them from their situation at birth they are snatched from prejudice. Once more one sees the truly revolutionary nature of Rousseau's work.

Rousseau talks of a 'natural education' in connection with all this. Once more we run into difficulties about this word 'natural'. The concept of education appears to require that something be supplied which would otherwise not be gained. 'Natural', on the other hand, would seem to deny the necessity for supplying anything and hence to make a strange companion for 'education'. Would not the best of educations consist in allowing things to take their own course? Indeed, Rousseau does use many negatives with respect to what is educative for the young child, and this presents us with the idea of 'negative education' which is quite as puzzling a term as 'natural education'. The problem is not completely unravelled in *Émile* (if it is ever completely unravelled). One must follow Rousseau's intention and move on to *The Social Contract* to tackle these paradoxes.

Having obtained his pupil and scholar, Rousseau now begins to use his acute observation to outline the characteristics of childhood. Long before the age of 'scientific' psychology this man was able to make generalisations of a kind which will still stand examination today. The psychological dominates everything in the account, and not always to the benefit of the consistency of some of the arguments which underpin the work. For example, with reference to the account of how to eliminate fear of, say, loud noises, there is some ground for accusing Rousseau of contradicting himself by recommending that one works from the contrived to the natural. Children are brought to a condition where they can experience thunder without alarm by arranging for a series of prior experiences of lesser noises of progressively greater impact. This is surely strange. If children are allowed to regard thunder as a sort of sporadic meteorological accompaniment to living one wonders why they should come to fear it if it is natural not to do so. And why they should not fear it if it is natural to do so?

This underlines again the fact that 'natural' is a concept that one can use as one chooses. The emotion of fear does not, it seems, fall within the concept in this instance at least. The ruling is that all fear is disadvantageous. Rousseau makes no distinction between fear and caution as a consequence. Of course, the latter involves a degree of rational appraisal which should not be expected of the very young, but Rousseau appears to require the elimination of caution at any stage. One could object to this by contending that caution does not involve fear but merely refers to a degree of care. One could go further than this, however. If one talks of caution in respect of such unpredictable phenomena as violent thunderstorms, or the traffic of a busy street, it could be argued that a degree of fear is very justifiable. No degree of care can guarantee one's safety.

The value of Rousseau's work in drawing attention to the importance of the senses in the business of learning has been pointed out, but the above indicates that this emphasis can also be misleading. One can demonstrate this by referring to Rousseau's discussion of the sense of smell. It becomes obvious that he fails to notice that the connection between smell as a sense and the source of the smell is by no means as easily grasped as, say, the connection between an object and the sight or touch of that object. This leads him to the dubious proposition that the *sense* of smell develops later than the other senses.

Secondly, and leading on from this, ruled by the notion of unfolding patterns of nature within us, Rousseau gives the impression that there are smells which are noxious of themselves. This is another dubious proposition. Our reaction to a smell is largely determined by the sort of associations which adhere to the source of the smell. What 'develops' late therefore is not the *sense* of smell but the degree of *learning* required before a smell is classified as pleasant or unpleasant. A certain gain in concept-formation is requisite to this. Indeed, Rousseau makes just this point in the second book when he explicitly states that training the senses is 'not solely a matter of use' for the reason that 'we neither touch nor see nor hear with any understanding but that we have been taught to do so' (Chapter 2, page 75).

The importance of concept formation and the result of the conflation of what is involved in it with what is involved in merely sighting, hearing, smelling, etc., continues to cause tangles in the argument. This is particularly true when Rousseau comes to a discussion of language. The vital point is that concepts are essentially public and rule governed: sensation is not. A child, a dog and a bird may all sight the same object, but they do not see it as the same thing. The child may see it as a ball. It is unlikely that the dog will and improbable that the bird could. The point increases in pertinence once one considers the relatively small part of language which merely functions to name material objects. Concepts such as 'same' or 'and' can be employed only after we have learned the conventions for their use, and these are much more complex than labelling or naming by using words like 'dog'. They are not acquired through the senses in any way that might be suggestive of the way in which one could come to acquire the convention of calling a particular object a dog. One cannot see, or smell, 'and', nor in a strict sense can one even hear an 'and'.

These are considerations which create difficulties for the acceptance of Rousseau's claim that there is a 'natural language' (which is a quite different claim from asserting that language is natural to man of course), for it is clear that Rousseau supposes this language to be essentially affective, to do with the communication of feeling.

We can be sorrowful or enraged and be known to be so without the use of language: we can be soothed or mollified by vocalisations of one sort and another which either do not include the use of words at all or do not rely upon words *as* words. (Think of 'There there then—never mind—ah'.) But we can admit this and still question the validity of Rousseau's analysis. It does not follow from the above that, when a child feels a need—say for food—and cries as a consequence, that, in so doing, he *asks* for help as Rousseau would have us think. It is one thing to identify a casual connection between the discomfort of muscular action in the stomach walls and crying; it is quite another thing to build into the crying implications of intention and purpose which are essential to the business of asking, begging or imploring. The casual connection is likely enough, but we should be very careful before according to a new-born infant an understanding of what it is to ask, beg or implore. The prerequisite to such an ability is surely experience and learning.

One clue to the muddle might well be the fact that Rousseau does not attribute differentiations of kinds of distress to the infant. 'All misfortunes bring to him but a single feeling of sorrow.' This observation is, in fact, irrelevant to the point at issue; indeed, if anything, it merely points up the error. It is the nurse then who must interpret. This cry of the young infant is an indication of hunger; that an indication of distress of some other sort. If there is this utter lack of differentiation in the infant, how can one assert any purpose in the cry unless one will go so far as to assume that the purpose is to provide the nurse with a task of interpretation! If one cannot, then it is difficult to see how one can subsume the cry under the category of language at all.

Since the muddles in Rousseau's position are by no means fully exhausted at this point and must be further examined, it is timely to point out the value of his work in case one loses sight of the fact that deficiencies are worth noting only in that which has a value. The entirely valueless can be dismissed without examination.

Rousseau attacks the idea that infants cry for 'the devil of it'. His use of the phrase *des vices naturels* when coupled with this carries the attack farther to counter the notion of original sin. Children cry because they lack an essential or are in pain; the cry is therefore to be heeded and not to be ignored as a first manifestation of the sinfulness of man. In a state of total dependence the child lacks all ability to remedy its own distress. We should take all steps to facilitate his progress towards strength and independence, but, at the same time, recognise his needs and meet them until and unless we know him to be capable of doing so himself. To adopt any other course is to corrupt his innocence and to turn his prayers into commands and threats. There would seem to be much good sense in this.

Returning now to the problems arising in connection with a natural language, perhaps the most serious of these is that it leads Rousseau to put a restriction upon the extent to which an adult engages in conversation with a very young child. Now a great deal of recent work serves to show that one cannot overestimate the gain that results when children are talked to freely. Rousseau is consistently guilty of underestimating this, probably because what he really, and justifiably, wishes to attack is the treatment of young children on a basis which assumes that they should understand all that is said to them. This and other problems are further discussed in the following chapter in relation to the text itself.

In many commentaries on Rousseau's book about educating a child much is made of his identification of stages of growth and the distinctness of each stage from the next. Much has been said about his insistence that the child is not an adult in miniature. No doubt this is all to the good. It is also a modern truism.

It is the contention of this writer that the essential arguments which Rousseau wishes to further are somewhat different from these particular and important insights and that they are all contained in the first of the five sections of the work. This commentary has therefore been founded on that section. For the rest, and the value to be found in the rest, the reader could not do better than to read *Émile* for himself.

Has the work of an eighteenth-century writer any relevance for the present time? Could one find an urging in favour of education according to nature in the day of space travel? It is proposed to allow the reader his own conclusions to these questions, but it is of interest to read the words of a North American Professor.

> The planet itself is now a little school. It's like being back to primitive times again. Then nature was education. You learned from nature around you. In this audio-tactile world it's happening again— only this time it won't be haphazard.[1]

[1] *From* Sunday Times *weekly review 13 August 1967. The Hunter Davies Interview with Professor Marshall McLuhan.*

Chapter One

'ÉMILE'—CENTRAL IDEAS

Almost at the very beginning of the book Rousseau states the basic premiss to the whole of the work.

> Everything is good as it comes from the hands of the Author of Nature: man meddles with it and it deteriorates. (I) 5. (V) 5.

This is the error that man invariably and universally makes.

> Even man himself is required to learn his paces just like a horse and must conform to the whim of his master just as must the trees in the garden. (I) 5. (V) 5.

From the basic premiss two important guiding propositions can be obtained. Rousseau states them as follows:

> (i) What we call wisdom is slavish prejudice.
> (ii) Every one of our customs bring us into servitude, constrain and compel us. (I) 13. (V) 10.[1]

Victim of all this is the infant. He is unaware of the wrongness of the treatment he receives from birth at the hands of elders previously enslaved and fettered by custom, and, in any case, is incapable of raising effective protest. Consequently, he becomes enslaved and fettered in his turn, and so perpetuates the pattern of which he is a product. Distortion begins at the beginning of life.

> Midwives profess to improve the shape of the child's head by moulding, and we allow them to do it! It appears that our heads lack perfection as fashioned by the Author of Nature. They have to be improved in looks by nurses and made over internally by philosophers!

Rousseau provides a first taste of irony here. He adds:

> The Caribs are far more fortunate.

[1] *Editor's numbering.*

The comment is intended to make a contrast between the simple and the artificial, and is of the kind which has given rise to the 'myth of the noble savage' for which Rousseau is generally and rather unfairly blamed. However, Rousseau does elaborate constantly upon the difference between fashionable French society and the simpler one of distant islands.

> Hardly has the child left the womb, before it has had a chance to stretch its limbs, this freedom is denied. Swaddling clothes are wrapped about him, his head is fixed, his legs stretched out and his arms secured to his sides. (I) 13/14. (V) 10.

This is what was to be found as common practice in France and in the section of that society which could conceive the notion of importing a German water dog and clipping its hair about the muzzle so that it bore a resemblance to the wig and beard of the owner's rival or enemy. But of the Caribbeans it was possible to notice that:

> They are tall, strong and well proportioned men even though they have not received the blessings of such great care for their future bearing when new born. (I) 15. (V) 11.

The attack is directed against the works of man in what Rousseau sees as a misguided social organisation dominated by artifice. Corrupted by such an environment man's meddling is inevitably to the detriment of what was originally good.

> ... he upsets everything, he mars it all, he prefers the deformed and the monstrous: he will not leave anything as nature made it. (I) 5. (V) 5.

A new fault in French society is now pointed out; a new deviation from the pattern of nature. The motive for the practice is also provided for inspection.

> Ever since mothers have shunned their prime responsibility and have proved unwilling to feed their children themselves, babies have been trusted to the care of hired nurses. These women, discovering themselves to be acting as if they were mothers of children they did not bear, are mostly interested in saving themselves labour. A child without swaddling clothes must be watched over all the time but when it is swaddled it can be left to cry. As long as no-one notices the nurse's disregard and providing that the child does not injure itself who cares? (I) 15. (V) 11.

Building upon this, Rousseau paints a horrifying picture of callous neglect by substitute mothers engaged to relieve 'gentle mothers' (women of wealth), of the encumbrance of the children they have born, so that they may the better devote themselves to the social round.

He attacks first from one direction and then from another. Where motherhood becomes a burden, the woman as wife becomes untrustworthy. Husbands seek consolation with other women.[1] As for the unfortunate infant, even if the hired nurse does provide the infant with milk, the doing so remains a paid service. The child therefore lacks what it requires above all.

> Other women, or even other animals, could provide the milk the natural mother can provide, but there is no substitute for the love of a mother. (I) 17. (V) 12.

Could not the nurse come to love the infant she is paid to nourish? Rousseau does not deny this possibility, but immediately points out two vital objections to this possibility as an acceptable alternative. Firstly, to be a wet nurse it is necessary that the woman should herself have but recently given birth to a child of her own.

> How can a woman be a good nurse when she is a bad mother who will feed another child in place of her own? In time she may become one; custom will over-rule nature, but before the nurse feels a mother's love for her charge the baby may die a hundred times. (I) 17. (V) 12.

Secondly, suppose this quasi-maternal affection to have developed in the nurse for the child she is hired to suckle; what when the task is completed? Is the natural mother now prepared to divide or to abdicate her claims upon the affection of the offspring? Can she face this?

> She will see her child loving another more than herself; receive what affection he has for his own (actual) mother as a favour while his duty is to love his nurse. Is not affection properly given where a mother's care has been received? (I) 17. (V) 12.

Rousseau does not see this as likely of the actual mother. Instead the child is taught to regard his nurse as a privileged servant. Once her function is fulfilled the nurse herself is no longer encouraged in her contact with or affection for the growing child she sustained in early infancy.

> The mother expects to resume her place and to undo the damage done by her own neglect by cruelly casting off the nurse. But she

---

[1] *And the women they find it with are simpler women who live in the country. Rousseau continues the comparison between the fashionable and simple.*

makes a big mistake; the child is made into an ungrateful foster child not into an affectionate son. The mother teaches him ingratitude. As he is now brought to despise the nurse he will eventually despise the mother. (I) 17. (V) 12.

Ingratitude instead of affection; scorn in place of respect; this is what Rousseau lists as the cost of displacing that which is natural to man. But suppose that we now find a mother who does not farm her child out to a wet nurse? It is not to be supposed that all is bound to be well in this case.

A woman who does not neglect her maternal duties may, on the other hand, be excessive in her care. She may make an idol of the child and, by doing so, increase his weaknesses by trying to prevent him realising them. She protects him against every painful experience, thinking to shield him from the power of nature by doing so. She fails to understand that, by shielding him from slight inconveniences, she stores up for him all sorts of adversities to be encountered in the future. She does not see that it is barbaric to lengthen the time of his weakness when he must suffer the consequences later. (I) 19. (V) 14.

It is plain from this that Rousseau does not protest against hardship befalling the infant. But the practice of swaddling the infant brings discomforts and detriments which are totally unnecessary. Furthermore, in suffering the unnecessary the child is prevented from experiencing those discomforts and hardships which *are* necessary.

Observe nature and follow the way she traces for you; she is ever urging children to activity; she hardens them by presenting them with all kinds of difficulty; she teaches them very early what it is to suffer and know grief. (I) 19/20. (V) 14/15.

This seems dour counsel and not easily accepted. It would appear that the loving mother is urged to place her child at risk. The natural requires it.

Do you not realise that attempts to improve upon nature's handiwork only destroy it; her cares are wasted? (I) 19/20. (V) 14/15.

Once we accept this we are the more easily convinced that the adversities of nature do not consist in accidents, nor are the buffetings of blind chance of no value. Since human life is bound to bring many dangers, those who are best equipped to survive them are those who have faced them from the outset. We should not upset this pattern by mistaken solicitude.

A child can tolerate changes which a man could not; the muscles of the former are malleable and soft and take without strain what bent is given them; those of man, being harder, no longer alter without violence the habit they have taken on. (I) 19/20. (V) 14/15.

Our first response to this argument may exclude reflection upon the state of medical knowledge in Rousseau's day. It may therefore appear to be curiously lop-sided, dwelling upon the structure of the human body alone rather than upon the diseases which affect it. The argument has its curiosities, but we should be less than fair to Rousseau if we did not take into account how little was known of the origin of disease and the treatment of ailments in the eighteenth century. People were subjected to the technique of bleeding as a cure for the most extraordinary things—anaemia, for example! Rousseau's contention that contemporary knowledge was seriously deficient is a valid one; so much so that one cannot altogether dismiss his claim that it is better to leave well alone than to profess understanding in the way the fashionable doctor tended to do. Rousseau is positively contemptuous of such men.

> For myself, I do not know of what ills we are cured by the doctors, but I do know that they infect us with many deadly maladies; cowardice, faint-heartedness, credulousness and fear of death.... Medicine is all the rage these days and no wonder. It is the diversion of indolent and unoccupied people who do not know what to do with their time and pass it preserving themselves.... Such people as they require the doctor who will flatter and threaten them and give them the only enjoyment to which they are susceptible—that of not being dead....
> (Just) as I will have no call for doctors myself I would call none for Émile unless his life was in evident danger, for then the doctor could do no worse than kill him. (I) 29/31. (V) 21/22.

Medicine, then, is one of the fashions of society and to be shunned.

> The sole aspect of medicine which is of use is hygiene; yet hygiene is less a science than it is a virtue. Temperance and work are the two true doctors of a man; work sharpens his appetite and temperance forbids abuse of it. (I) 31. (V) 23.

The whole criticism is carried upon a distinction between adversities encountered as a necessary consequence, from which nothing but good can come, and those incurred by man's departure from the path of nature.

> The lot of man throughout life is to suffer. Pain is the means of his preservation. Happy is the childhood which knows only physical ills. These are much less cruel and distressing than other ills and but infrequently lead to renunciation of life. One does not kill oneself as a consequence of twinges of gout; it is anguish

of mind which produces despair. We pity the lot of childhood when it is ourselves we should pity. Our greatest ills are of our own making.

It is now a little difficult to see quite what Rousseau would wish to happen should it befall a child that none of these beneficially adverse circumstances which he has suggested come his way. To urge the mother to *arrange* for painful experiences would make hay of his own condemnation of such practices as swaddling. He can avoid the dilemma only by supposing a number of things as natural which are by no means inevitable, even when no steps are taken to prevent their occurrence. For this to be possible the term 'nature' takes on considerable flexibility and imprecision. We become puzzled. Where is the 'golden mean' of child care? Just what must the wise mother provide, what guard against and oversee? How must she proceed?

To all these questions Rousseau's first answer is a bleak one. The reply is essentially negative.

... the most important thing is to prevent anything being done.

The first duty of parenthood is to love and nourish; the second to refrain from positive action, to avoid all forms of imposition or direction. However well intended our efforts to guide him, the outcome is predestined to produce disaster.

An infant passes six or seven years in this manner in the hands of women, victim of their caprice and of his own, and then when they have taught him something or other, that is to say after his memory has been burdened with words he is unable to understand or with things which, to him, are only good for nothing ... he is handed over, helpless, into the hands of a teacher who puts the finishing touches to the artificiality already implanted in him.... Finally, this child, drudge, and tyrant, full of learning but destitute of feeling or judgment, equally debilitated in body and mind, is sent out into the world, there to display his ineptitude, his arrogance and all his faults. (I) 21. (V) 16.

However, we may now return to two earlier points: first, that nature is for ever urging children to be active, and second, that hygiene is a useful part of medicine. That the parents do nothing positive and the tutor follows them in this, does not abandon the child to aimlessness. That the machinations of doctors are worse than useless does not imply a complete disregard for personal care. The adult has a function in the child's life.

A child should be unaware of superiors other than his father and mother, or, for want of them, his nurse[1] and he who brings him up; but even two may be one too many, yet this division is inevitable and all that can be done in remedy is that the man and the woman having governance of him be in such accord on his behalf as to act as one. (I) 34. (V) 25.

Within a home having this complete accord the twin principles of activity and hygiene provide the mother with her function. She herself must be healthy and of such a temper as to bestow upon her infant the care stemming from willingness, patience, gentleness and cleanliness. The last is considered at some length by Rousseau, and he injects into the discussion a reiteration that all things should conform to the natural.

... this precaution of making the water lukewarm (when bathing the infant) is not indispensable; indeed multitudes of people bathe their newly born children in the rivers or the sea without fuss. (I) 37. (V) 27.

That the water should be warmed at all, even for the new-born infant, is only necessary because the parents have been so softened by generations of artifice that the child's constitution is already enfeebled at birth. It is a concession to inherited mischance, one of very few that Rousseau is prepared to make.

As he grows up I would require that the child accustom himself to bathing in water at all supportable degrees of heat and sometimes in water of all possible degrees of cold. (I) 38. (V) 27.

Curiously, Rousseau sees the business of bathing the child in extremes of temperature of water to be instrumental in enabling him to withstand equally violent fluctuations of air temperature.

Thus, after having been accustomed to withstanding the diverse temperatures of water, which is a dense fluid, touching us at more points and affecting us more than air, we shall be all but unaware of change in air temperature. (I) 38). (V) 27.

He would have children much in contact with the open air from birth. He would also have him provided with space.

Men were never made to be huddled together as in ant heaps, but dispersed over the world to cultivate the earth. The more they crowd together the more they corrupt each other. Physical ailments as well as evil thinking and feeling are the inevitable effects of living closely massed. Of all the animals man is least fitted to live in herds. The breath of man is fatal to his like, this is true both literally and metaphorically. (I) 37. (V) 26.

[1] *Rousseau contends that she who nurses is the real mother.*

Whether the infant is to be cared for by nurse or by mother, it is from the town and not to it that mother or nurse should go with the child. Once there, Rousseau returns to reiteration of an earlier prohibition and to the recommendation to allow activity. (We must not put some special meaning to this term when reading Rousseau. Unlike, say, Dewey the idea of activity is in no way tied to learning or to a way of learning.)

> Do not restrain the child from the moment it first draws breath. No caps, bands and swaddling clothes. Let him be garbed in loose fitting clothes which leave his limbs at liberty and are neither too heavy so that they check his movements nor so warm that they prevent the air having access to him. Place the child in a wide, well padded cradle within which he can move with ease and safety. When he grows stronger allow him to crawl about the room; let him develop and exercise his little limbs and you will see him gain in strength daily. Compare him with the child who has been tightly confined in swaddling clothes and the difference in rate of progress will astonish you. (I) 38. (V) 27.

We now have a rather more clear picture of the role of the mother / nurse. At the same time we learn that there is no golden mean of guidance or direction. The child learns where no one teaches. He must accumulate a capital of sensory experience unhindered by precept.

> —the new born infant is straightway a pupil not of a tutor but of nature. (I) 39. (V) 28.

The mother must be vigilant that nothing interferes with the promptings of nature in the young child. She is therefore not a mere bystander nor yet only a source of sustenance. All the artifice of society will seek to disrupt these promptings, and this must be thoughtfully counteracted.

> One sees the eyes turning towards the light, and if the light comes from the side, naturally take that direction. Take care then to turn the head also, so that the child does not come to squint. (I) 42. (V) 29.

It would seem that even a windowed room can be a snare. It is an artificial environment productive of habits of custom.

> The sole habit one should permit to a child is that of acquiring none; carry him no more upon one arm than upon another; do not allow him to use one hand more than the other, to eat, sleep, or do anything at particular times; to be unable to be alone by night or by day. Prepare him now for the use of his liberty and his strength, allowing his body its natural habits, so that he is always

master of himself and able to do all that he wishes once he has a will of his own. (I) 30. (V) 42.

Establish no habits then, but let the body's 'natural habit' be the governing factor. Rousseau gives some further indication as to what is to be meant by this, proceeding by a number of steps, all of which suppose the impulsion of needs which are in the nature of the child.

He wishes to touch and to handle everything; do not oppose him in this restlessness for it provides him with a vital apprenticeship.... It is only by movement that we apprehend what is of ourselves and that which is not of ourselves, and it is only by our own movement that we acquire the idea of distance. Lacking this idea the infant indiscriminately reaches for objects approximate to him and those a hundred paces away. (I) 31. (V) 44.

As the first condition of man is one of misery, want and weakness, so his first sounds are plaints and tears. The infant feels his needs and is incapable of satisfying them; he implores help from others by his cries ... he has only one mode of speech as it were, just as he has but one distress, for, in the undifferentiated state of his senses, he does not distinguish their diversity of impression, therefore all misfortune engenders a single feeling of woe. (I) 46. (V) 32.

What Rousseau calls the child's 'real need' is not the possession of the object but the ability to crawl or walk. This real need, aroused *by* the object rather than *for* it, can become a need for possession— a corruption of the real need—unless we are cautious. A number of warnings are given about the care to be taken to avoid merely gratifying the child.

Children begin by being assisted but can end by being served.

Capriciousness develops out of need and the first seeds of prejudice and obduracy are sown.

This is the way whereby children become troublesome, tyrannical, imperious, depraved and unmanageable. (I) 47. (V) 33.

Everything appears to forbid interference with the working of the activity principle in the child. Whatever it brings him we cannot improve upon it.

At the same time as the Author of Nature gives to little children this fundamental activity, he takes care that it shall not be harmful by limiting their strength. But as soon as they come to see the people about them as instruments they can depend upon to act for them, they place these others in servitude to supplement their own weakness. (I) 49. (V) 34.

We now arrive at four maxims which provide a guide for the mother in her care of the child. In fact they have a far wider application than this and underpin the whole of Rousseau's account of education.

(1) Far from having superfluous strength, children are not sufficiently strong to meet all that nature asks of them. They should be permitted the use of all that they possess, for they will not abuse it.

(2) Aid and supplement them in their lack, whether in understanding or in power when it is a matter of physical necessity.

(3) Confine your help to the meeting of genuine need, granting none at all to serve whims or unreasonable desires, for these do but torment the child and are not originated in nature.

(4) Study with care their language and gestures, so that, they being of an age when they cannot dissemble, one may distinguish among their desires those which are direct from nature and those which are not. (I) 50. (V) 35.

At this point we turn to a consideration of the father's role in the upbringing of children. No radical change of policy is involved; the same basic principles apply.

Rousseau has said that the mother who does not suckle her child, who allows another to nourish him, to be the object and the provider of affection and care, fails to be the 'real' mother. What is sauce for the goose is sauce for the gander. Just as—

> ... the true nurse is the mother so the true tutor is the father. They should be agreed as to their functions and also as to their way of working, so that the child passes from the care of one to the care of the other. He will be better brought up by a wise if limited father than by the most able teacher in the world, because zeal makes up for lack of skill better than skill can make up for lack of zeal.
>
> But pressure of business; one's work; one's obligations! Ah yes! Doubtless of all these the last is that of being a father! It is not surprising that the man whose wife finds it beneath her to nourish the fruit of their union, himself disdains to bring him up.... If the mother is of too delicate a constitution to nurse the child the father will be too occupied with affairs to be his teacher. (I) 22. (V) 16.

Rousseau now cites Suetonius on Augustus, 'the master of the world'—who taught his grandsons to write and swim. Does this happen in eighteenth-century France?

> But what does this rich man (of France) do, this family man who is so occupied with other things that, by his own account, he

must abandon care of his children? Why; he pays someone else to remedy the lack which he should see to.

Oh false heart! Do you believe that you can buy another father? Do not deceive yourself. It is not even as if you had provided a master for your son. You have given him a flunkey. In due time he will make a second of the child himself. (I) 23. (V) 17.

The painful business of displaced affection is again warned against.

Their absent children, dispersed to boarding schools, convents, and colleges, transfer to other places the affection they would have had for their homes, or bring to their homes a habit of caring for nothing at all. Brothers and sisters will be ill at ease with each other; when in public places they will be polite to each other but act as if they were strangers. (I) 22. (V) 16.

Rousseau now injects himself into the writing. He constructs a tiny dialogue embodying the reactions of the ensnared father to the analysis just presented to him. Rousseau answers his queries.

Who then can educate my child?
I have told you—you, yourself.
I am unable to do so.
You cannot! Then you must get a friend to do so. I can see no other way. (I) 23. (V) 17.

By this device Rousseau declares himself as someone standing beyond the situation and viewing it clearly but with a certain contempt for the enmeshed individual.

In begetting and providing for children, a father has done no more than a third of his task. To his species he owes men; to society men able to live with others, and to the state, citizens. Any man able to pay this threefold due and failing to do so is culpable, and the more so still perhaps when he only part discharges it. If he cannot perform the tasks of a father then he forfeits the right to be one. No plea of poverty or of work or of position secures a dispensation from the duties to support and educate his children. (I) 23. (V) 17.

In all this the hireling nurse, disinterested and possibly callous in her treatment of the child in her care, is matched by the hireling tutor, a sort of intellectual flunkey. Neither are in any way a benefit to the child. They cannot fulfil the functions they must perform.

There are occupations so noble that they cannot be engaged in for payment without showing an unfitness to undertake them.

Hence Rousseau, in the snatch of dialogue given above, advises the father to call in a friend to take the place which is properly his if he persists in protesting his own inability to fill it. One must procure a person who stands as an equal and who *desires* to fulfil the function tragically pronounced as impossible for the actual father.

> There is a great deal of talk about what is required in a good tutor. The first thing I require, and many other things follow from it, is that he be not a man for hire. (I) 23. (V) 17.

Now can Rousseau point to the sort of man who, as friend and equal, will serve as tutor? In ironic agreement with the difficulty here exposed, Rousseau turns the question into a further indictment.

> A tutor! Oh how sublime a being! Truly in order to train a man like this one must either be a father or, oneself, above men. This is the office you will happily leave to hirelings.

There is cold comfort for the father in the increasing starkness of his answer.

> The more you think about it the more difficulties you will encounter.... Can this rare mortal be found at all? I cannot say. In this time of degeneration who can know what degree of wisdom and goodness the heart may attain? ... It seems to me that the father who can understand the worth of a good tutor ... will assume the task himself rather than go to the greater trouble of acquiring a suitable substitute.... Nature has already done half the work of fitting him to do this. (I) 23. (V) 17.

We are returned to the vital point—the real nurse is the mother, the real tutor is the father. Nature has it so. Search for an alternative that will not distort and deprive and you run into more difficulties than it seems possible to overcome.

But surely there must be one man at least who could fulfil the saintly role of tutor; the man who can outline what is involved. Rousseau is quick to counter this inconvenient point.

> I am too aware of the nobility of the tutor's office and of my own lack of fitness for such a position ever to take it up, whoever made me the offer. That he would be a friend who did so is but a further reason for refusing. Having read this book I doubt that many would be tempted to offer me such a post, and I pray that anyone who still would will save himself the trouble. (I) 24. (V) 18.

Neither will he depart from the negative answer he has given to the father's inquiry by pointing to 'better men' than himself—say monks. However, since it must be supposed that nature's design is discernible (or talk of doing things according to nature would be without force), Rousseau must be able to offer something. He does this by pointing out that it is in the nature of being a father that half the work of discovering what it is to be a good tutor is done for one by the promptings of nature. He can then contend that—

> If we examine the nature of his duties we shall discover the sort of man he must be. (I) 24 (V) 17.

By this move Rousseau avoids an impasse—

> Although unable to fulfil the more useful task I can, however, attempt an easier one. Following the example of many others I will take up the pen in an endeavour to say what should be done since I cannot do what should be done. (I) 24 (V) 18.

We must not lose sight of this as we read on through the five books of *Émile*. We may otherwise forget that the use of the first person does not indicate any reference to Rousseau's actual experience or to his intentions as an actual tutor. It is a device of style convenient to the author. This is not what Rousseau can do, has done or will do, but what should be done to be consistent with the argument and if there is to be any improvement in the social and political lot of man. (One might wish that all educational messiahs had this honesty.)

With this established the following does not appear to be quite as remarkable as it would otherwise have done.

> I do not speak here of the qualities of a good tutor. I suppose them to exist and myself to be endowed with all of them. As you read this book it will be plain how generous I have been to myself. (I) 25. (V) 18.

The tutor in *Émile* is a construct, a sort of prototype of what a man should be as father and/or tutor. He has now to be provided with employment, a fact which brings new problems simply because all that has gone before states the need of the child for his own parents and denies the need for a tutor as such at all. Rousseau adopts another expedient.

> I have therefore taken leave to give myself an imaginary pupil, whilst supposing of myself the age, health, knowledge and all the talents requisite to fit me to educate him from the time of his birth until he needs no other guide than himself. (I) 25. (V) 18.

However, an imaginary child does not escape the need for (imaginary) parents. Rousseau has not yet managed to counter or to evade the difficulty. But the step allows of a second.

Émile is an orphan; irrespective of whether he has a father or mother. Charged with their duties I am possessed of their rights. He should honour his parents but obey me. This is my first and sole condition. I must add what is no more than a corollary to it; we must never separate except by mutual consent. This clause is essential and I would have tutor and pupil regard their fate as one ... when they realise that they must always be together they must needs love one another and will therefore learn to do so. (I) 27/28. (V) 20.

Rousseau avoids the problem by creating a vacuum. *Émile* is, or is as if an orphan; that is to say that, whether he has living parents or no, if he is to have a tutor, then it must be that they surrender him up immediately and completely. A bleak prospect? Rousseau is in no doubt it is, but there is the alternative course. Rousseau has already laid this out for us in a passage previously quoted.

It seems to me that the father who can understand the worth of a good tutor ... will assume the task himself. (I) 24. (V) 17.

A golden mean or middle course? As with the nurse/mother discussion there is none for Rousseau. There is now an added significance to the comment in the snatch of dialogue that 'I see no other way'.

There are to be no flaws *in* Émile as he comes to the tutor.

I would not take on a sick or enfeebled child even if he was destined to live until he was eighty years old. I would not want a pupil destined always to be a burden to himself and to others, solely concerned with keeping hold on life, and whose physique was an impediment to the development of his mind. (I) 29. (V) 21.

Shortly after this Rousseau launches his attack upon doctors and the practice of medicine. The whole business of illness or handicap is to be attributed not to nature but to the handiwork of man. Nature can be the only remedial influence. At this point, too, Rousseau is able to make his usual comparison with a simpler (better) society; or so we might expect.

To discover what ways are the most preservative of life and health one has only to refer to the ways of races who are known to be superior in strength and longevity of life.... It requires little thought to come to the inescapable conclusion that long life is the attribute of men who take most exercise and who know what it is to work hard and be tired. (I) 32/33. (V) 23.

It is surprising that a footnote here does *not* refer to the simpler society but only to the simpler man; not to the Caribs, the Peruvians or even the Romans but to one Patrick O'Neal, an Englishman supposed to be born in 1647, to have married a third wife in 1760, to have drunk only small beer, lived exclusively on vegetables—and lived to be more than 130 years old. One wonders how many such examples could have been found in England of that time.

No flaws then, and an orphan. Now to be an orphan or as if an orphan requires that there be a nurse (or the mother must act as nurse).

> With the beginning of life our needs begin also. The newly born child must have a nurse. If his mother will fulfil this duty all is well and good; her instructions will be given to her in writing.... It is to be supposed that her wish for the welfare of her child and the esteem she bears for the one to whom she has entrusted him will cause her to be attentive to the wishes of the tutor. (I) 32/33. (V) 23.

If the mother does not act as nurse—

> I shall not act on the advice of the doctor attending the birth but take care to choose one for myself. (I) 33. (V) 24.

Rousseau has now set up the situation, but, so far, he has left the tutor as a shadowy if saintly character. He intends that the rest of the book shall reveal what he must do and how he must go about it, and so inform the reader as to the qualities which must be possessed by this man. However, Rousseau does not leave the reader to his own powers of divination and insight to quite this extent.

> Contrary to the general view I think that the tutor to a child ought to be young; as young as it is possible to be and yet be wise. I would wish that he could be a child himself if it was possible, for then he would be companion to his pupil, obtaining his confidence and sharing his amusements. There is nothing in common between childhood and age; the distance is too great. There is no possibility of a firm attachment between people so far apart. Children sometimes flatter old people but they do not love them. It is also thought desirable that the tutor should already have educated one pupil. This is too much. One man can only educate one pupil; if two are necessary before success can be assumed, by what right can he undertake the education of the first? ... your man may change his pupil every five years or so; mine will have just one. (I) 25. (V) 19.

Building upon this, Rousseau now makes a very important conceptual distinction, albeit in a somewhat unclear manner—

> You make a distinction between 'teacher' and 'tutor'.[1] Another

---

[1] *In the original the terms are* 'précepteur' *and* 'gouverneur'. *'Vous distinguez le précepteur du gouverneur: autre folie!'*

folly! Do you make a distinction between 'pupil' and 'disciple'?[1] (I) 26. (V) 19.

Working back from this rhetorical question, he now seeks to demonstrate the folly of acting upon a distinction between 'teacher' and 'tutor'.

(i) There is but one science to be taught to children; it is the knowledge of the duties of man. This science is unitary ... it cannot be divided up.

(ii) I would sooner call a master of this science a tutor than a teacher because he concerns himself less with telling the pupil than with guiding him. He should not give rules; he should allow them to be found[2] (I) 26. (V) 19.

From (i) one may move to the dangers of making separations such as are made when man is not considered as man, the individual person, but as man, the citizen, subject or social component. For Rousseau the only one of these that has validity is the first; the introduction of these partitions—which smack of the modern notion of 'social role'—only serves to cancel out the whole. Then man becomes as a cipher.

A citizen of Rome was neither Caius nor Lucius; he was a Roman.

is to be contrasted with—

The natural man is all to himself; he is self contained and self sufficient, having association only with himself and his companions.[3] (I) 9. (V) 7.

Now since:
The man who is a citizen is not a unity but divided in himself, then his worth is to be measured by his affinity with the whole, with the society. Society must therefore change its character for it does not now permit the following condition.

To be of a unity as himself and always undivided within himself, man must act as he speaks, decide his own course and invariably pursue it. (I) 10. (V) 8.

Now immediately we divide this 'science of life' at the dictate of the false distinctions just outlined we lose sight of its unity and of

[1] *Rousseau makes use of* 'disciple' (*follower*) *in the original.* '*Distinguez-vous le disciple....*'
[2] *The passage is obviously not divided in this way in the original.*
[3] *Rousseau writes, 'L'homme naturel est tout pour lui.' To read this as* '*all for himself*' *would be misleading. Self-sufficiency is what is indicated rather than disregard of the interests of others.*

our own. The claims of society upon man as a citizen are the claims of fashion and custom which violate the promptings of nature in man as man. All the parrot cries about public duty and social philanthropy arise only because of the effect of this disastrous separation upon the moral goodness of man. They are useless counters to the corruption created in man by this division—useless because, no longer at one with himself, even his 'public spirited' behaviour is informed by an underlying and corrupted sense of his own individuality and selfish interests.

The requirement, then, is man as himself and not imprisoned within a 'social role'. However, the modern sociologists have made it abundantly clear that the notion of man in isolation is not a tenable one, that what is left after the removal of social roles and social influences is not the undefiled and perfectly self-contained but the incomplete and incoherent; incomplete in so far as all the evidence seems to point to man as a 'society-building animal'; incoherent in that language and communication develop within the context of 'society building', and do not precede it in a way which makes it plausible to think of these attributes existing and developing without their being a society of men. The distinction is therefore a false one and the concept of 'man as himself' not a feasible one if by it is meant man in social isolation.

Rousseau will be at pains to distinguish self-interest from selfish interest, the latter being a debased form of the former and totally predatory, exclusive of consideration of others. In the long run, he will argue, selfish interest is destructive of oneself. It banishes compassion, fellow feeling and tolerance, and these are vital to one's own survival among others. We see here the close link between the two works, *Émile* and *The Social Contract*.

Rousseau now turns his eye upon the educational agencies of the day, so steadily moving out from the close consideration of parental duties alone.

> I do not think of the ridiculous establishments we call colleges as public institutions. I do not count for much the fashionable education they give, because it faces two ways in attempting to achieve contrary ends, so achieving neither. (I) 10/11. (V) 8.

A footnote to this is of interest. The jibe about *risibles établissments qu'on appelle collèges* is not to be taken to mean that in these places (which include the University of Paris) there are no individual teachers who require no persuasion to the point of view Rousseau advances. Rousseau had some acquaintance with the teachers of the

University, and his comment is presumably one which is to indicate that there are some swans among the ugly ducklings. Why do not the swans act as swans therefore? Once more Rousseau foreshadows the twentieth century in that he points to the dreadful power of existing social influence. Until there is a methodological reform these men, as the rest, are shackled within the system, however inimical to them its ways. Yet even this is too optimistic. Things have gone too far—

> The public institution does not exist any more. (I) 10. (V) 8.

Conditions in society and of it are such that the only worthwhile idea of public education is no longer a practicable one. The model Rousseau takes here is that contained in Plato's *Republic,* which he denies to be a work on politics. It is *le plus beau traite d'éducation,* and since what it sets forth is not practicable in contemporary society, no existing institution can be of value—none of them preserve the unity of the science of the duties of man (qua man). We shall not find our tutor within them any more than, by Rousseau's account, we shall find a Socrates.

Upon this basis Rousseau sees the tutor to be guide and source of reference rather than dispenser of wisdom and fount of origination. However, this will not mean that the tutor does not teach, if by 'teach' we mean something other than the giving of mere exposition. This can be exampled by leaping into Book III of *Émile.*

> Taking a stone I make as if to put it down in the air. I open my hand and the stone drops to the ground. Of the watching Émile I ask, 'Why does the stone fall?' (I) 199. (V) 140.

By any modern account (and surely, too, if we regard Socrates to be a teacher) the tutor is here teaching.

This much said of the tutor, Rousseau turns to a further consideration of Émile himself. Many additional points are now added and discussed concerning the proper person to be educated. First, it is plainly stated that exceptional innate qualities are not demanded.

> Were I able to choose I would select an ordinary sort of child such as I suppose Émile to be. Only the ordinary man stands in need of education and his education alone can serve as a model for all like him. The rest must find their way in spite of this. (I) 26). (V) 19.

Another stipulation is rather more startling. The subject is to be selected from among the rich. The reason for this is a complicated one.

Make your selection from among the wealthy. The poor man has no need of education; his situation in life is forced upon him; he can have no other. Conversely the education brought by the situation of the rich is least fitted to serve either the individual or society. Whereas, a natural education should prepare a man adequately for any human condition. (I) 27. (V) 20.

Émile is thus to come from a well-situated family. To remove him from it is to save yet another person from becoming slave to prejudice, a fate already spared the child of the peasant, since fashion and artifice play little part in the hard-working lives of the poor countryman of France. They grow up the more kindly for it. In contrast, as Rousseau points out elsewhere in the first book:

> It is a misfortune of the rich that they are cheated on all sides; it is no surprise that they think badly of all mankind. (I) 33. (V) 24.

Rousseau now addresses himself to the general consideration of the manner in which, unless in some way prevented, Émile and any other child will learn as he grows. It is this aspect of *Émile* which is most celebrated, and justly so. Rousseau's remarkable insight into the psychological factors which influence learning anticipate much later work by clinical and experimental psychologists.

To begin with, it might be fruitful to note again what is said by him of the results of interfering with the child's learning as nature would have him do, to recall all the criticisms to be made of faulty mothering and schooling which have led up to this point in the book—'allow him to crawl about the room'—'compare him to the child who has been tightly confined in swaddling clothes' 'The sole habit one should permit to a child is that of acquiring none' (page 38). The governing dictum is always that the child is 'a pupil not of a tutor but of nature', and one should assist only 'when it is a matter of physical necessity'.

What follows now can be contrasted with usual practice. It is particularly important to notice what is *not* done for the child or to him that he should learn and what *is* done by the child of himself from which he learns. This is the essential of the contrast.

> We are born with senses, and from birth we are affected in many ways by the things about us. As soon as we are, so to speak, conscious of our sensations we tend either to seek again or to avoid the objects which produce them. (I) 9. (V) 7.

The human being seeks or shuns according to the pleasure or pain to be gained or suffered, that is to say according to the sensations which are experienced. At least this is so in the first instance.

Later, rational considerations of utility and of morality modify this pattern, but not in infancy.

> We are born able to learn but knowing nothing. The mind, imprisoned within a body of imperfect or half formed organs, is not even fully aware of its existence. The movements and cries of the new born child are merely mechanical, devoid of understanding and volition. (I) 40. (V) 28.

But the existence of the purely mechanical does not go far to explain learning—

> There is no direct connection between the muscles of the stomach and those of the arms and legs such as would cause him to take one step or to reach out a hand even if food was all about him. (I) 41. (V) 29.

It seems clear that Rousseau must introduce something other than mere mechanism into the account. Furthermore, this must be a connection involving the conceptual.

One might think that understanding is a necessary condition for concept formation, but this is not the case for Rousseau. The first processes of learning are of an order between the merely mechanical and the employment of concepts. One might cite him thus—

> (a) Living and feeling creatures are always learning.
> (b) Experience goes before instruction.
> (c) When the child is able to recognise his nurse he has learned a lot.

Of these (c) is the first to cite an *instance* of learning. It is therefore a pity that he does not elaborate upon his use of 'recognise'. We need not take him to mean that the child recognises the nurse in any sense more complicated than that he identifies her as 'the same again'. He may be supposed to do nothing so complicated as recognise nurse as nurse. This is a negative point, however, and it leaves us still unclear as to what is necessary before 'recognise' is used.

This lack of precision in the argument is convenient for Rousseau's account. A previous and heavily stressed contention from Rousseau has been that the child's true nurse is the mother, but now we may wonder whether, if the child *cannot* recognise nurse as nurse, it really matters if the nurse is the mother or not, particularly if we disregard the effects upon the mother and the nurse in the case[1] and consider only the child put to a loving nurse. Of course, the use of 'recognise' might be differently interpreted than as above. Rousseau's position is elastic enough to bend to any criticism, but a

[1] *See page 33.*

position so pliable as this is bound to be uninformative, since such contrary interpretations may be accommodated within it.

What *is* clearly stated is the coincidence of learning with experience. From this Rousseau takes his reader through an account of processes in learning which now have such names as association and conditioning. He shows their significance in the formation of attitudes, a concern of great moment to his whole work.

Children who are brought up in well ordered households where no spiders are tolerated have a fear of spiders which persists throughout their lives. I have never seen peasants, whether men or women or children, who possess this fear. Why then cannot the education of children begin before they can speak or understand, since just the selection of objects which are presented to them is sufficient to make them timid or courageous? I would want a child to become accustomed to see new things; ugly animals—ones quite disgusting and bizarre—but gradually and from a distance, until he becomes accustomed to seeing them and their like and then to seeing others handle them, and is able to do so himself. If, during his childhood, he sees toads, snakes, and crayfish without experiencing fear, he will know no fear at the sight of any animal when he is fully grown. He should not then be afraid of anything he sees during his life.

All children have a fear of masks. I begin by showing Émile an agreeable mask of a pleasant countenance and arrange for someone to put it to his face. I and everyone present laugh at this, the child with the rest of us. Little by little I get him used to less agreeable masks and finally to hideous noses.

If I have managed my gradation well, far from being afraid of the last mask, he will laugh at it just as he did at the first.

If Émile must become acquainted with the noise of firearms I would first burn a percussion cap in a pistol. This short-lived flame, this kind of lightning, will delight him. I should repeat the performance but adding a touch of powder. Little by little I should increase the charge. (I) 43/44. (V) 30/31.

And so on until we come to bombs, cannons and 'the most terrible explosions'. The whole notion of this 'battle training' sounds somewhat odd, but it is the technique adopted and the processes of learning which are inferred that are worthy of note. With respect to the former, it could be suggested that the artificial or contrived is used to assist orientation to the natural, say to violent thunder claps. Rousseau has an answer.

I have observed that children are rarely afraid of thunder unless the peals are such as to be terrible enough to hurt the ear. Otherwise the fear only comes to them if they realise that thunder can hurt or kill sometimes. When reason thus occasions fear allow the usual to reassure them. (I) 44. (V) 31.

A second point of interest in this example is that Rousseau will not allow that there can be such a thing as 'healthy fear'.

Slowly and carefully one brings man and boy to be fearless of all things.

He now turns from the formation of attitudes to the child's manner of acquiring knowledge. (The following is not continuous in the original.)

At the commencement of life, when the memory and imagination are as yet inactive, the child is only attentive to that which actually affects the senses. His sensations are the first data upon which he can build knowledge and understanding ... (therefore) ... since he is attentive only to sensation it suffices at first to show him very clearly the connection between his sensations and the objects which cause them. He wishes to touch and handle everything. Do not oppose him in this restlessness; it leads him through a very necessary apprenticeship. It is thus that he acquires experience of the heat or coldness, hardness or softness, heaviness or lightness, of material objects, to judge of their size, shape, and all their sensible qualities, by looking, touching and listening, but, above all, by comparing sight with touch, estimating by sight what sensation objects will give to the fingers. (I) 44. (V) 31.

In a footnote to this Rousseau states that smell is the last of all the senses to develop in children. The second section of the Introduction to this book points out that this is a very doubtful statement, suspect because it quite misses the importance of concept formation. Oddly enough, however, the very next paragraph is all but exclusively concerned with concept formation.

It is only by movement that we acquire an understanding of things which are separate from ourselves, and it is only by our own movement that we acquire the idea of distance. (I) 44. (V) 31.

Precisely what is involved in concept formation is by no means easy to grasp. This has been a little more fully dealt with in the Introduction in connection with the point above. Whether Rousseau himself realised the central importance of concepts is a little difficult to guess, but it would be rash to accuse him of complete ignorance on this and absurd to accuse him of lack of understanding of the very words he uses; words such as 'idea' which must be used very loosely indeed if they are not to carry the implication of conceptualisation. Given this, it would be equally absurd to accuse him of no understanding of the child as he comes to use words. Language consists in concepts, and Rousseau opens his discussion of language development with a statement which surely makes this plain.

All our languages are works of artifice.

Yet we find that he is stating that something is faulty here, not that something is a matter of fact. There is a language, *the* language which we have abandoned; a language given by nature.

For a long time men have sought to find out if there was a natural language, common to all men; without doubt there is one. It is that spoken by children before they make use of words. This language is not articulated but it has stress, tone and intelligibility. We use our own language (of art) to the point of neglecting this language altogether. If we study children we shall very soon learn it again from them. (I) 45. (V) 32.

Now, in the original, we find the words:

—sans doute, il y en a une; et c'est celle que les enfants parlent avant de savoir parler.

The temptation is to translate much as in the passage immediately above. An alternative might be both more accurate and revealing of a problem.

undoubtedly there is one: it is that which children speak before they know how to speak.

This is nonsensical without an accompanying assertion that there is a language common to all men and used from birth, one consisting in sound rather than words, in intonations and sound intensities and variations, which can be still further augmented before vocalisation of words is even thought of. There is gesture.

... which is no less forcible. The gestures are not made by the feeble hands of the infant but by his features. It is amazing what expressiveness is possible to such immature faces. (I) 45. (V) 32.

Tears, cries and facial expressions are therefore among the basic components of language and available to the smallest of infants long before there is any question of his use of that sort of language which is the result of artifice, namely the use of words.

Rousseau departs here from the common use of 'parler'. Cassell's *French–English, English–French Dictionary*[1] gives the following meanings for the word (among others):

To speak, to talk. (Where 'to talk' is to mean articulate utterance.)
To discourse, to converse
To have meaning

[1] *Ed. E. A. Baker, Cassell & Co., 25th edition, 1954.*

Now Rousseau explicitly states that:

(*a*) The natural language does not consist in words.
(*b*) It is not articulate in the sense normally conveyed by that term.

Beware of words then; treat them only as a substitute for natural language and not as words at all.

Nurses are our masters in this language; they understand all their charges say; they respond to them and conduct dialogues with them which both follow perfectly. They might pronounce words but these words are perfectly useless; it is not the meaning of the word that is understood but the way in which it is spoken. (I) 45. (V) 32.

Although the vocalisations of the very young lack all the rules and conventions normally considered essential to language, it is folly to dismiss them as meaningless or as expressions of innate wilfulness. They are vital signs and indications of the condition of the infant. This is to say that Rousseau's natural language is a language of affect; its basis is purely emotive. At the age Rousseau deals with in Book I of *Émile* the 'age of reason' or of reasoning has not dawned in the individual.

It is by reason alone that we distinguish what is good and what is bad. Conscience, by which we come to love the one and hate the other, although independent of reason, is unable to develop without it. Before the age of reason therefore, we do good or bad without knowledge of so doing.... (I) 48. (V) 34.

Failure to recognise this leads to the malpractice of precipitating the child into the language which is the result of art, instead of permitting him his own 'natural' language and allowing him to come to the use of words of his own accord and in his own way and time. That time is not before there is a beginning of the development towards reason.

Their organs (of speech) are as yet numb and dull, only allowing them, little by little, to imitate what they hear spoken ... and it is by no means certain even then that they hear correctly that which they attempt to reproduce. I do not disapprove of a nurse amusing a child with songs and with happy and varied expressions of voice, but I do disapprove when she bombards him incessantly with a multitude of useless sayings of which he understands nothing but the tone of voice employed. I require that the first things said to him for him to understand, should be few, distinct, often repeated; and that the words spoken should have reference to observable objects which can be shown to the child immediately before the words are spoken. The unfortunate tendency that we have of employing words of

which we can understand nothing, develops earlier than we think.
The school child must listen to the verbiage of the class teacher, just,
as in his swaddling clothes, he heard the babblings of his nurse. It
seems to me that it would have been greatly to his benefit had he
been left knowing nothing of either.

Dawning apprehensions crowd in on us when we think about the
way language and speech came about, and of the first speech of
children. Whatever we may do they all learn to speak in the same
way and all philosophical theorising is quite futile here. As a first
point, they have, so to speak, a grammar of their age, with a
syntax and rules vaguer than our own, and if one pays careful
attention one will be astonished at the exactitude with which they
follow certain analogies, very misguidedly perhaps, but very regularly.
Anyway they are only objectionable because they are harsh or dis-
cordant, or because they happen not to be common usage. I have
just heard one poor child fiercely admonished by his father because
he said *Mon père irai-je-t-y.* Now it is clear that the child was following an analogy more correctly than our grammarians, because since
they say to him *Vas-y* why should he not say *Irai-je-t-y?* . . .

Is it the fault of the poor child if we clumsily deprive a phrase of the
determinative adverb '*y*' simply because we did not know what to
do with it? It is unforgivable pedantry and an utterly superfluous
regard for rectitude to pull the child up on every petty fault against
normal usage, for they need no such correction; they do the same
for themselves given time.

Always speak correctly yourself when with them; see to it that
they gain more pleasure from your company than from anyone else's,
and rest assured that the way they speak will be modelled unconsciously on the way you speak, without any correction from
you. (I) 53/54. (V) 37.

One is bound to notice in this an obvious inconsistency with the
previous statements about a natural language in distinction from
a language resulting from art. When Rousseau permits himself to
say that a mistake might be made he is tacitly admitting that language *is* rule-governed and that any person's use of it may be referred
to standards of correctness. Furthermore, the latter part of the passage concedes the fact that some rules may be intrinsic to the
language and of first importance. Others may have the status of
mere fashion, affectation or pedantry, and they can be ignored
or broken without offending against the first kind of rule. This
distinction is obscured, however, because Rousseau also appears to
lump all rules, etc., together under the pejorative term 'custom'
and then to use an example which offends against the second sort
of rule rather than the first.

The persuasive force of the example tends to blind us to all this.
C

But the example itself can be regarded with great suspicion. Suppose, for example, careful and kindly correction had been given rather than the severe scolding of the child. Would it not give pause for thought? Secondly, it is extremely unlikely that the father admonished his child for a fault in grammar as such. It is much more likely that his desire to see (or hear) his son as a 'typical' Frenchman caused him to upbraid him for a deviation from a familiar convention of speech rather than any concern for the structure of language. Of course this does not affect the facts of the case, but it does affect the interpretation. It is manner of speech that is central, and not concern for language. Talk of grammar and so forth is peripheral. Thus the example, and Rousseau's whole argument at this point, attacks affectation and defects of clarity in *speech* (mis-speaking) without distinguishing them from errors of construction, from *what* is said. This failure is continued; the discussion of language *per se* becomes a discussion of pronunciation and enunciation only.

> ... people press children to speak as if afraid they would not learn to do so of their own accord. This ill judged pressure produces a directly opposite effect to that which is desired. They speak later and more confusedly. (I) 54. (V) 37.

Now here, 'more confusedly' might, as yet, refer to both the manner of speaking and to the content, to what is said. This is less true of what follows, however.

> ... the extreme attention given to all that they say makes good pronunciation unnecessary and as they therefore scarcely bother to open their mouths many children acquire, and keep for the rest of their lives, a dreadful pronunciation and confusion of speech which makes them all but unintelligible.

And still less true again of the subsequent paragraph.

> I have lived amongst peasants and I have never heard any of them speak with uvular distortions, neither man nor woman, girl or boy. Now why? Are peasants' organs of different construction to our own? Of course not; but they are differently exercised. In front of my window there is a knoll where the children of the neighbourhood gather to play. Although they are some distance from me I can distinguish perfectly all that they say and can take good notes for this book. Always what I hear deceives me as to the age of the children. I think I hear the voice of ten year olds, but I look out and see children of the size and features of three to four year olds. (I) 54. (V) 38.

Rousseau is now talking exclusively of manner of speech and use of voice.

> The reason for this (difference) is that, until they are five or six, town bred children, brought up within doors and under the eye of a governess, have no need to do more than murmur to secure attention; as soon as their lips move people strain to hear them. People say words to them which they repeat incorrectly; whereupon, by dint of the most effortful concentration these same people who attend them always, make out what it is they are trying to say rather than what, in fact, they do say.
>
> One notices, it is true, that those who commence to speak late never speak as distinctly as their fellows, but it is not because they are late speaking that they have this embarrassment; it is because they are embarrassed that they speak late. If this is not the case why should they speak later than others? Have they less occasion to speak, or been less encouraged to do so? On the contrary; the disquiet that their retardation produces once it is remarked, leads people to torment them into stammering out something even more than they urge those who talk at the more usual time, and this misdirected eagerness is very likely to make the speech of the child confused when, with less haste, they would have had time to bring it to a greater perfection. (I) 54/55. (V) 38.

Now *tourmenter* can mean variously: torment; torture; worry; pester; tease. We need not, therefore, think of mockery alone. This fact is not made clear in Rousseau's account. For example, one may worry (i.e. torment; pester; or tease) a child with deliberate intent, but a child may also be worried by someone or something when there is no intention that this should happen. Rousseau does not do justice to this possibility. As a consequence, his comments could well be productive of uncertainty and hesitance in those dealing with young children. Anxious to avoid any imputations of ill intention towards their charges, they might restrict themselves to the point where a wise restraint is transformed into a regrettable lack of proper encouragement.

A second query concerns the logic of the position. Could a child unable to speak be brought to know that he was being teased *about not being able to speak*? Once more there is the need for the distinction between language *per se* and speech which Rousseau has so far tended to ignore or pay scant heed. In this case we need to know whether it is problems of a physiological and neurological nature which are involved in the discussion or problems of comprehension—a psychological concern. Rousseau recognises this duality of problem category in the following:

Children who are pressed to speak have not time to come to pronounce well nor to understand properly what it is they are <u>made</u> to say,[1] whereas when left to themselves they begin by perfecting themselves in the pronunciation of the easiest syllables,[2] then, lending them, little by little, additional meaning by the use of gesture, they give their own words[3] to you before they receive yours. In this way they do not acquire words from others until they have been understood. There being no urgency to use them, they begin by carefully noting what sense you give them, and when they are sure of this then they adopt them as their own.

The greatest evil of precocity of speech by little children is not that the first conversations one has with them and the first words that they say lack sense, but that they attach other senses than the proper meaning without our knowing or understanding this to be so.

Thus, although they appear to respond to us quite correctly, each speaks to the other without understanding of what has been said. It is the frequency of this sort of ambiguity that causes surprise at what children say to us; we attach ideas to their words which they had never thought of. This inattention on our part to the true meaning that their words have for the children who speak them, appears to me to be the cause of their first mistakes,[4] even when they are corrected, continue to exercise an influence upon their thought for the rest of their lives. Later on I shall have more than one occasion to give examples which make this clearer still. (I) 57/58. (V) 40.

This is a valuable paragraph. It is being increasingly realised that much depends upon early linguistic interchange with infants; this being particularly the case for concept formation. Balanced against this, in Rousseau's account, is his apparent bar to just this exchange in some of the earlier passages. Modern work in this field stresses the conceptual impoverishment resultant upon hearing not too many but too few words, not too complex but too simple a language structure. This is to be compared with—

[1] *Editor's underlining. Is 'made to say' descriptive of a possible compulsion?*

[2] *This contention is a very doubtful one. What will count as 'the easiest syllables'? One could make the statement self-validating by defining the easiest syllables as those which children first utter. The point then becomes uninteresting. Secondly, it is questionable whether the modern psychologist would want to say that children practise syllables rather than utter sounds.*

[3] *'Their own words' must mean 'our words' which they imitate, or else the position must be that words develop from the child, a strange notion.*

[4] *—me parait être la cause de leurs premières erreurs;—The word 'erreurs' can be taken to mean 'slip', 'mistake', 'fallacy'. The word 'idée' can be taken to mean 'thought'. It is difficult to choose quite the right word in translation.*

Restrict the vocabulary of the child as much as it is possible to do. It is most unfitting that he should have more words than he has ideas; and that he should know how to say more things than he can think. (I) 58. (V) 40.

That the child is not to be teased or tormented to speak seems to force us to another extreme; that of restraining the child from using words. Surely a sort of artifice or custom is now being *proposed* not opposed here. Secondly, if the child is *using* words it is difficult to see how he could be said to have words but no ideas, for he could not be said to be using words as words in that case. The same error informs the following:

I believe that one of the reasons why peasants are generally more accurate of judgment than townsfolk is that their stock of words is less extensive. They have few ideas but these are clear and well applied. (I) 58. (V) 40.

But the final paragraph of Book I is as relevant today as when it was written. It is a reminder for us, but perhaps a revelation in Rousseau's day, that the first years of life are of tremendous importance and characterised by an astonishingly complex developmental pattern.

The first developments of infancy occur in a number of directions simultaneously. The child learns to talk, to eat, to walk, all about the same time. This is the first stage of life. Until then he is little more than what he was before birth, without feeling or thought, hardly possessed of sensations, unaware of his existence. (I) 58. (V) 40.

Acquire all this and infancy is passed. There is a child rather than an infant. From this point Émile is specifically considered as exemplifying childhood, and the tutor is plainly one familiar with what has been set out in general in the first book.

It would be a radical mistake to imagine that Book I merely discusses or describes infancy. The matter of the first part of *Émile* is the ground plan of ideas by which the tutor works in all his practices until Émile is ready to leave his care. All the guiding principles are set out in it. Much of the rest of *Émile* will consist in the application of them in different contexts, child as opposed to infant, youth as opposed to child and so on. Hence the treatment of this section has been full.

Chapter Two

A CHILD BEFORE A MAN

At the beginning of the second book of *Émile* Rousseau restates that the first stage of life is to be called infancy and that, once the multi-directional developments mentioned at the close of the first book are showing themselves in the child's behaviour, then that stage is completed. That this is so does not involve any change of approach to the education of the child. It might so far have been thought that Rousseau's objection to the treatment of children in infancy is merely a protest against a *too soon* attempt to subject the child to formal teaching. We are quickly disabused of any such idea upon entering Book II. What has been said in Book I is to be the pattern throughout; and this pattern is essentially contra to the generally accepted one of an increasingly formal schooling.

> Our pedantic mania for teaching leads us to teach children the very things they could learn better for themselves and to forget to teach them the very things that we alone could teach them. (I) 60. (V) 42.

The revolutionary character of the work is summed up in the general directive—

> Do precisely the opposite to what is usual practice and you will have hit upon the right way of going about your task. (I) 83. (V) 58.

The customary way; the bondage of fashion; these are the shackles which bind and corrupt, which thwart the already implanted and infallibly good urgings of Nature in the human being.

> In what then does human wisdom consist and where the way to true happiness? A simple curtailment of what we desire is no answer because this could have the effect of lowering our aspirations to an extent which did not allow our full capacities to be realised.

It is no better to extend the scope of our faculties if our desires are also extended to outstrip them; we should only be the more miserable. We must seek to close the gap between our desires and our powers until there is a perfect correspondence between what we wish to do and what we are capable of doing. (I) 63. (V) 44.

The only man who can obtain his own ends is he who has no need of the aid of another to achieve what he wills; it is therefore the case that the greatest of all blessings is not authority but freedom. The truly free man is he who only wishes for what he can do and only does what he wishes. This is my fundamental rule. One has only to apply it and all the rules of education flow from it. (I) 69. (V) 48.

Plainly the concept of education as Rousseau uses it is in no way one restricted to particular fields of intellectual activity nor can it in any way be thought of in terms of formal schooling in areas of knowledge. The term is used to indicate a comprehensive orientation of the individual to his total situation as he grows. It is informed by the notion that the promptings of nature within him are both strong enough and better than any external prescription. It is therefore the educator's job to act as a sort of midwife to the 'perfect' man emerging from the growing child.

Before human prejudices and human institutions have impaired our natural inclinations the happiness of both children and adults consists in the use they make of their liberty but the liberty of the former is limited by their own weakness. Whoever does do as he wills is happy if he is self-sufficient and this is the condition of man in a state of nature. He who does as he wills is not happy if his desires exceed his powers as is the case with children in a state of nature. Even in this state then, children enjoy only an imperfect liberty similar to that enjoyed by grown men in social life. To the extent that any of us are dependent upon others we are to that extent weak and wretched. We were intended to grow to be men; laws and the dictates of society plunge us back into infancy. (I) 70. (V) 49.

It will be seen from *The Social Contract* that Rousseau has in mind here the exercise of arbitrary authority over men by kings or despots concerned only with the gaining of their own ends, albeit in the name of the state. In the same way *The Social Contract* makes it plain that interdependence in the sense of the one assisting the other in some sort of brotherly affection is not quite what Rousseau is referring to in the above by the use of the expression which has here been translated as 'dependence'.[1] Perhaps the extreme case

[1] *Namely the phrase* ne pouvant plus se passer des autres.

Rousseau has in mind is that of the slave's dependence upon his master and owner for everything, including his very life.

There are two sorts of dependence; that upon things which is according to nature, and that upon men which is according to society. Dependence upon things possesses no moral implications and so does no violence to liberty and engenders no evil; dependence upon men, having no order or limitation, gives rise to all kinds of evils with the result that master and slave become equally depraved. If there is something that can be done to remedy this evil in society it is the substitution, through law, of the general will as a real force, superior to the whims of any one individual. If the laws of nations possessed the same invariability as the laws of nature, not be vanquished by any human power, then dependence upon men would become dependence upon things, for then there would be a reuniting within a republic of all the advantages of a state of nature and those of the civil condition; the freedom which preserves a man from evil would be conjoined with the morality which raises him to virtue. (I) 70/71. (V) 49.

This passage is plainly a statement of the general basis of *The Social Contract*. It is now applied to the education of children.

Preserve the child within a condition of dependence upon things alone; this is the way in which you can follow the course of nature in his education. Oppose nothing against his indiscreet desires but the physical obstacles they must overcome and the punishment which his own actions will bring about and which he will recall on similar occasions in the future so that, without forbidding him to refrain from wrong doing, he will, nevertheless, be prevented from so doing. His experience or his impotence will serve in place of the observance of law. Take no heed of his demands, provide only what he needs.

It is then not a question of obedience when he acts or of tyranny when you act for him. So he will come to know equally what it is to be free in his actions and what it is for you to be free in yours. Supply only that power on his behalf which he requires for freedom and not for imperiousness so that he receives your assistance with some humiliation and seeks to dispense with it the moment he can aspire to serving himself without assistance. (I) 71. (V) 49.

The principle of activity is now reasserted.

Nature strengthens the body and allows for growth by her own means and one's only care is to do nothing to thwart this. One should never require a child to be still when he wishes to move about nor to move around when he wishes to remain still. When the child's will is not impaired by our shortcomings then they wish for nothing that is not useful. Let them leap, run about and shout just as much as they wish. All their movements serve the needs of their constitution if it is to be strengthened. However, one should be distrustful of such of their desires as they cannot themselves fulfil and which must be answered for them. Always one must distinguish with care the true, the natural need, from the fantasy need, the acquired desire from that which comes from the abounding life I have spoken of. (I) 71. (V) 50.

Still early on in the second book Rousseau now extends his stricture concerning the vocabulary of the child, applying it to the new phase of growth he has identified.

Constantly guard against giving the child vain formulas of politeness which serve him as magical incantations with which to subjugate all about him to his will and to obtain what he wants instantly. The fashionable education of the rich leaves nothing undone which will make its subjects politely imperious by versing them in modes of address such that no person will be so bold as to resist them; their children have neither the tone nor the manner of suppliants. They make their requests arrogantly; more arrogantly than they issue their commands, as if they were more sure of being obeyed. For them, 'If you please' means 'It pleases me', and 'I beg of you' means 'I order you'. Admirable politeness, which succeeds in changing the meaning of words so that nothing is spoken which is not a command! As far as I am concerned I would prefer Émile to be rude rather than arrogant; I would much prefer that he says, as a request, 'Do this' than that he says 'I pray you' as a command. It is not the words which he uses which are important but the meaning he attaches to them. (I) 72. (V) 50.

Another reassertion is that concerning the necessity for the child to endure certain categories of hardship.

—the liberty I grant to my pupil amply compensates for the slight inconveniences to which he is thereby exposed. I see the little rascals playing in the snow, blue and benumbed, scarcely able to move their fingers. They could take themselves off to a warm place but they do no such thing; if one compelled them to do so they would be a hundred times more conscious of hardship than they are of the rigours of the weather.

Do you imagine that true happiness is possible to anyone who is not acting according to his nature, and is it not contrary to this condition when one removes from the situation all the misfortunes to which the species is naturally subject? I would say that if one is to experience the great goods one must experience also the small misfortunes; this is his nature. Too much bodily comfort corrupts the morals. The man who knows nothing of pain and sorrow can know nothing of compassion nor of the sweetness of commiseration; his heart could be touched by nothing, he would have no social sense, he would be a monster among men. (I) 73. (V) 51.

It is important to notice that the notion of 'dependence upon things' includes enduring the exigencies of the situation in which the child finds himself. They wish to play snowballs; their hands must get cold, and they must accept this. No one rushes out to provide them with gloves or to usher them indoors to thaw out their fingers for them, nor does one discuss the pros and cons of desiring to play snowballs in the first instance, seeking to dissuade them from their objective. Important to all this is the contention that to reason with a child of this age is useless. For Rousseau, reason is a faculty, and it has not yet developed.

I return to matters of practice. I have already said that your child should obtain nothing from you merely because he asks for it but only when it fills a need, neither should he act out of obedience to you but solely from necessity. Thus words of obedience and command are outlawed from his vocabulary but those of effort, of necessity and of inability and constraint, are to be given an important place therein. Before the age of reason it is not possible to form any idea of morality or of social relations; one should therefore avoid employment of words which express them for fear that the child will attach to them false ideas which people will either allow to persist or be incapable of rectifying. The very first erroneous notion that becomes fixed in his head is the germ of error and of evil and it it is for this that one must constantly be on the alert. Arrange things so that what strikes his attention are things of the material world and his ideas are thus confined to the sensations; if this is not done it is certain that he will either take no notice of you at all or will gain fantastic notions about the moral world of which you speak which will prove ineradicable throughout his life.

Locke's principal contention that one should reason with children is much in vogue at present but I do not think that it achieves anything to its credit when it is followed; it seems to me that I have seen no more stupid children than those who have been reasoned with in this way. Of all the faculties of man, reason, which is, as it were, an amalgam of all the other faculties, is the most difficult and the last to develop, and yet it is proposed to develop the earlier through it! The end product of an education is the making of a rational man and here you claim to educate a child through his reason!—If children were aware of what it is to reason there would be no need to educate them. (I) 76. (V) 53.

Rousseau now puts forward an illustrative dialogue purporting to show the futility of reasoning with a child. At the same time he incorporates into this example of what not to do, the ideas of obedience and of command which he has previously proscribed. His claim is that most *leçons de morals* must take this shape. The reader must be the judge of this.

He may well come to the conclusion that, although this is an example of what not to do, it is by no means the only way to do what is being attempted. It should be remembered that Rousseau can tailor his examples to fit his case.

Master	(It is to be noticed that 'tutor' is not used.) Do not do that.
Child	And why must I not?
Master	Because it is a wrong thing to do.
Child	Wrong! What do you mean by wrong?
Master	It is forbidden you.
Child	What is there about this wrong that I am forbidden it?
Master	You will be punished for having disobeyed.
Child	I can do it when no one is looking.
Master	You will be watched.
Child	I shall hide myself.
Master	We shall inquire what you've been doing.
Child	I shall lie.
Master	You mustn't tell lies.
Child	Why not?
Master	Because it is wrong.

Observe; the circle is inevitable. Go farther and the child will not understand you. (I) 78. (V) 54.

In a further stricture a little later on Rousseau returns to the twin evils of making too much of sophisticated language and of supposing the faculty of reason to be operative. He conjoins this with the dangers of restrictions upon the liberty of the child by too much direction (which, for Rousseau, adds up to any direction at all).

Give your pupil no kind of verbal lesson at all; he should receive nothing but experience. Inflict upon him no sort of punishment because he does not comprehend what it is to be at fault, and do not require that he begs your pardon for he does not understand what it is to give offence. Not yet having a capacity for moral judgment he cannot be said to act immorally and so merits neither chastisement nor reprimand. I can imagine that the frightened reader will immediately compare this child with others; he will be mistaken in his judgment. The continual control put upon these children excites their vivacity—the more they are constrained when under supervision the more they are turbulent the moment they can escape; they make every effort to compensate themselves for the restrictions you place upon them.... I believe you will have achieved much if you have managed to hold your tongue. (I) 81. (V) 56.

Then follows the celebrated passage from which is to be derived the notion of 'negative education'.

> May I make so bold at this point to reveal the greatest, the most important, the most useful rule of all in education? It is not that one should save time but that one should lose it. The ordinary reader must pardon my paradoxes; they are unavoidable when one thinks for oneself and, whatever you might say, I prefer to be a man of paradox than of prejudice. The most dangerous period of human life is that between birth and twelve years of age. It is the time when errors and vices germinate and when there is yet no instrument for their destruction. When the instrument is available the roots are so deep that it is too late to tear them out. If children sprang straight from their mothers' breasts into the age of reason then the usual form of education would be suited to them, but the natural progress requires an altogether contrary approach for there to be accord between growth and education. (I) 82. (V) 57.

> The first stages of education ought to be purely negative. It does not properly consist in instructing in virtue or truth but in preserving the heart from vice and the spirit of error. (I) 83. (V) 57.

How is this to be achieved? In answering, Rousseau now states another celebrated notion; namely that education consists in serving growth.

> Take precisely the opposite steps to the usual and you will nearly always do well. As they have no wish or thought to make the child a child but a university scholar, most fathers and teachers feel it can never be too soon to correct, reprimand, cajole, threaten, induce, instruct and reason. Do better than this; act reasonably and do not reason with your pupil. Above all do not force approval of what he actually dislikes because in this way reason is constantly associated with distasteful things so that it becomes distasteful to him to reason before he is even able to understand what it is to use reason. Exercise his body, his organs, his senses and his powers but keep his mind idle for just so long as you can.... Finally just what lessons are really necessary to him? Guard against giving today that which could be deferred until tomorrow without danger. (I) 83. (V) 58.

> Nevertheless I am far from thinking that children possess no sort of reason. On the contrary I notice that they reason very well in all things that have a bearing upon their immediate and perceived interests. But it is on the extent of their understanding that people are misled so that they are attributed with knowledge they do not have and so urged to reason about that which they do not comprehend.
> Yet another mistake they make is to attempt to turn the attention of children to considerations which in no way affect them, such as interest in their futures, of their happiness when grown to manhood

and the opinion of people will have of them when they are grown up; talk which, when directed at those quite unpossessed of foresight, has absolutely no significance. Now all the enforced study of these poor wretches concerns subjects which are utterly foreign to their minds. You must judge how much attention they are able to give to them. (I) 104. (V) 72.

It seems then that Rousseau is not saying that the child is unreasonable but that the *faculty* of reason is not developed. What is to be meant by 'reason' in the light of all this is a little difficult to explicate. We can say what is NOT to be meant; namely dealings in abstractions. These must await the development of the FACULTY of reason and the enlargement of experience.

Now it is demonstrably sensible to exclude from a discourse with young children that which is beyond their comprehension simply because it is not within their experience in a way which cannot immediately be remedied. Rousseau precedes Dewey in pointing out that young children (and, perhaps, the not so young) find talk of their future adult responsibilities and rights to be within this category. But this seems to provide no ground for supposing this to necessitate the emergence of a faculty of some sort. Where the person is capable of structuring and forming concepts in relation to his 'immediate and perceived' interests (and this degree of 'abstraction' must be possible for such a state of affairs as Rousseau allows in respect of young children), then it would seem that they must be attributed with powers of reasoning which are precisely similar in kind though not in scope to those possessed by people at a later age.

In a footnote to the above passage Rousseau appears to recognise the difficulties in his argument for a faculty of Reason which develops subsequent to a time when he wishes to call children reasonable.

I have thought a hundred times that it is impossible in a long work always to give the same sense to the same word. There is no language which will furnish as many terms and turns of phrase as will match the modifications of our ideas.... Nevertheless I am persuaded that one can be clear for all the poverty of our language, not by attaching the same meaning to the same word in all instances but by ensuring that each time the word is employed the meaning to be given to it is sufficiently indicated by the ideas which are being expressed and that each sentence in which it is to be found serves as a kind of definition. (I) 104. (V) 72.

Now the attempt to deal with the troublesome business of reason has led Rousseau to give a general but suspect account of language. Yet the difficulty about reason is not cleared up, even to Rousseau's satisfaction. He returns to the problem again towards the end of the second book.

> In the books which follow I have to speak of the cultivation of a sort of sixth sense, called common sense, less because it is common to all men than because it results from the well ordered use of the other senses and instructs in the nature of things by unifying all their sensible characteristics. This sixth sense is not dependent upon a particular organ; it resides nowhere but in the mind and its sensations, which are purely internal, and called perceptions or ideas. It is by the number of these ideas that our knowledge is assessed; their distinctness and clarity determine accuracy of thought and the art of comparing one with another is what is called human reason. Thus what I term childlike or sensory reason consists in the formation of simple ideas by the combination of several sensations, and what I call intellectual or human reason consists in the formation of complex ideas by the combination of several simple ideas. (I) 174. (V) 122.

The passage outlines the approach to the education of the child until approximately twelve years old. The five senses are to be allowed full rein, and from their 'well ordered use' will grow or develop the sixth or faculty of reason. At the end of this period one should be able to claim that:

> ... we have led our pupil pleasurably through the area of the sensations to the limits of childlike reason; the first step beyond this point must be the step of a man. (I) 174. (V) 122.

Whether this elaboration goes any further towards establishing the development of a new faculty remains still doubtful. That a different KIND of judgment and a new mode of thinking may develop is more tenable; indeed, such a suggestion is central to Piaget's work in our own time. This fact can surely be as well accounted for by noting the obvious increase of skill necessary to handle this sort of mental performance. It presupposes a coming to know what it is to compare and to judge, etc., and this, in its turn, requires knowledge of what it is to classify and to categorise as well as an appreciation of the value of such activities, all of which it takes time to gain. It follows therefore that dealings in the 'abstract' are later. It does not follow that they herald the development of a new faculty that MUST produce such dealings as the phrase 'must be the steps of a man' implies. Given experience *and* such guidance and instruction as are necessary to the acquisition of skill in reasoning, it is likely that they will follow. Both Rousseau and Piaget share the fault of supposing the development to be inevitable. That this is not the case is clear enough. Ironically the social anthropologist can point to many examples to show this from the study of primitive societies. One would have thought of Rousseau as one who realised this were it not understood that his talk of man in a state of nature had no foundation in empirical investigation.

We may now return to what it is appropriate to put before children prior to development beyond the reason of sensation. Rousseau commences by issuing a number of prohibitions against particulars of what is the usual practice.

> People will be surprised that I count the study of language among the number of useless things in education but bear in mind that I am talking about the studies proper to the early years, and, whatever anyone says, I do not believe that, prodigies apart, any child truly acquired two languages before the age of twelve or fifteen years of age. (I) 105. (V) 73.

The reason for this returns us to the distinctions made in the passage concerned with the reason of a child in comparison with that of a man.

> In order to be possessed of two languages he must be capable of comparing the ideas in each, and how can he compare things of which he has hardly any understanding?
>
> In any study at all, without the idea of the thing represented, that which represents the thing is valueless. However, people always limit the child to these signs without being capable of bringing him to an understanding of things represented. It is thought that he is being brought to understand what the world is like but he is only coming to know what a map is, to know the names of towns, countries, rivers, which he does not conceive of as existing except on the paper where he finds them.
>
> It is even more ridiculous to make them study history. It is imagined that history is within their grasp because it only consists in a collection of facts. But what does one mean by this word 'facts'? Do you believe that the connections which produce facts of history are so simple to comprehend that the ideas formed from them present no difficulties in the child's mind? Do you believe that a true understanding of events is separable from an understanding of their causes and their effects and that the historical is so little related to the moral that the one may be understood but not the other? If you see the actions of men only as external and physical movements, what do you learn from history? Absolutely nothing; and this study, denuded of all interest, brings you neither pleasure nor instruction. If you wish to evaluate those actions by their moral implications, attempt to make those implications understood by your pupils, and

you will then discover if they are old enough to study history. (I) 106. (V) 74.

How, then, might one go about communicating moral understandings to young children? Rousseau turns upon the favoured notion that this may be done by embodying them in fables and cautionary tales.

> How can people so shut their eyes to the truth as to think of fables as supplying a morality for children without realising that the very plot and the amusement it engenders misleads them; that the seductions of the story are such that the truth escapes them so that that which is intended to make the instruction pleasurable is also that which prevents him profiting by it? Fables can instruct grown men but children must be told the naked truth. By wrapping it up one gives nothing but increased difficulty. (I) 110. (V) 77.

Rousseau takes as an example a fable from La Fontaine, making his own analysis and comment as to how children would see the story and what they would gain from it. His principal objections are that the language of the fable is subtle and informed by many stylistic devices quite outside the grasp of young children (how could they comprehend such a phrase as 'beside himself with delight' for example?), and secondly, that children identify with the characters according to their fortunes not according to the rectitude of their actions.

> In all the fables where the lion is a character, since he is generally the most splendid, the infant will be nothing but a lion, and when he oversees some sharing out of goods, well informed by his model, he takes care to reserve for himself the lion's share of all. But when the gnat vanquishes the lion that is another matter; then the child is no longer the lion but the gnat. He learns the way to kill by stinging to death those whom he cannot conquer in the open.

> When you provide them with contradictory teachings what fruit do you expect for your pains?

> Let us come to an agreement, M. de la Fontaine. So far as I am concerned I promise to read you of choice, to love you and to be instructed by your fables because I expect not to mistake their intent, but permit me to prevent my pupil from the study of a single one of them until you have proven to me that it is good for him to learn about things of which he can understand but a fourth part.... (I) 114/115. (V) 80.

If such an 'arrangement' can be made with M. de la Fontaine in respect of his work intended for mothers and children, then there

is warrant for a much more general educational precept applicable
to this age of child.

In thus relieving children of these duties I have relieved them of
the cause of their greatest misery, namely books. Reading is the
scourge of childhood and yet is the sole occupation we find to give
him. At twelve years old *Émile* will hardly know what a book is. (I)
116. (V) 81.

How and when will the child come to read if this policy is adopted?
Will he not remain for ever illiterate? Is it not imperative to begin
teaching him at the earliest moment possible? If not, when is it
time to give him this teaching? Are there not many intriguing and
pleasurable ways of teaching reading which will be of great interest
to the child as well as of great benefit to him?

People make a great to do about discovering the best method of
teaching reading; they invent special apparatus and systems until the
room looks like a printer's workshop. Locke advocates the use of
dice! Could a better idea ever be found! What a pity it all is!
Superior to all of this and constantly overlooked is the child's own
desire to read. Once this desire to learn is given to the child you can
dispense with your apparatus and your dice; any method is good
enough.[1]

Present interest is the great moving force, the sole sure persistent
guide. *Émile* sometimes receives invitations from his parents or friends
to dine with them or go for a walk or attend some public celebration.
These notes are brief, clear, plainly stated and well written. He must
find someone who will read it to him. This someone cannot always
be found just at that time; the same small effort to oblige is shown
him as he himself was prepared to give the day before. Time passes
and, with it, the opportunity. The note is finally read to him but it is
too late. Oh; if only he could have read it himself! Other notes are
received; so short, so interesting, and he wishes to decipher them
himself. Sometimes he receives help and sometimes it is refused. He
makes a tremendous effort and contrives to decipher half of the note;
it is something to do with taking cream tomorrow but he knows not
where or with whom. What efforts he now makes to read the rest!
I do not believe he has need of apparatus. (I) 116. (V) 81.

Rousseau then adds a cryptic comment to the effect that the above
analysis makes it quite unnecessary for him to comment on the
teaching of writing.

The notion of negative education is now somewhat more clearly

[1] *The word 'apparatus' has been used here to stand in place of the
original which reads,* on invente des bureaux, des cartes. *This is because
what is referred to are long-vanished techniques of historical interest
only.*

adumbrated for the reader. It consists in the provision of opportunities rather than of instruction, but it carries no implications of *inactivity* on the part of the tutor, who must constantly be making judgments as to what to arrange. There is, in fact, a very positive side to the business of judging when *not* to do something, for that is just as much a way of responding to the pupil as any other.

> Take an opposite course (to usual practice) with your pupil so that he believes himself to be the master when, in fact, you always have control. There is no form of control so complete as that which preserves the appearance of freedom, for thus one captures the will of the subject. This poor child, who knows nothing, has little power and understanding; is he not at your mercy? Can you not order everything that affects him in his environment? Can you not make of him what you please? Although he does not know it is it not the case that his work, his play, his pleasures and his pains are all in your hands? Without doubt he should do only that which he wishes to do, but he ought to wish to do only that which you want him to wish to do; he ought not to take a step that you have not anticipated or open his mouth to say that which you would not expect of him. Under these conditions he is able to devote himself to the physical activity appropriate to his age without stupefying his mind and, not requiring to devise ruses to escape irksome restrictions, can gain from his environment all that can contribute to his well being. You will be astonished at the subtleties of his endeavours to gain for himself the ends he makes his goal and how thoroughly he can enjoy himself unaided by the advice of others. When he is thus left the master of his own volitions you awaken no capriciousness in him. Obliged to do nothing that is not to his liking he shortly comes to do only that which he ought.
>
> His continual physical activity assists him in the development of reason about all his immediate and sensory experience to as full an extent as is possible for him, far more so than would purely theoretical studies. (I) 121. (V) 84.

From all this there emerges a picture of the function of education as an essential ancillary to growth according to the impulsions of the natural.

> The judicious man can maintain his proper place but the child cannot do this until he knows what his place is in the order of things. There are a thousand possible deviations and it is the care of those who have control over the child to keep him in his place; no easy task. He should be neither beast nor man, but child. Although he must not suffer through his weaknesses he must nevertheless feel his weakness. Although he must not be constrained to obedience he must realise his dependence. He is subject to others only because of his needs and because they are able to see better than he can what his

needs really are, what may further and what detract from his existence. (I) 69. (V) 48.

Education is to be according to nature and not according to the fashions and customs of a corrupted society. The essentials can be listed as follows:

(a) Inability to meet one's needs is the source of much, if not all, deviations from the natural.

(b) To the extent to which the educator eradicates this inability, albeit gradually, then he is educating according to nature.

(c) Self-sufficiency is to be thought of in terms of the development of capacities which meet true needs.

(d) True needs are those which arise for man in a state of nature. All else is 'caprice' and corruptive.

(e) Man's capacities develop in an ordered sequence, culminating in the development of the faculty of reason, at which point, and only then, theoretical studies become important together with such needs as to read, to write, and communicate at a distance. His natural mode of reaching this stage is through practical experience of the environment, both material and social. For this to be possible he should be allowed to conduct himself as an investigator within an environment carefully overseen and structured by the tutor.

We may now exemplify these points from the text.

In order to exercise an art it is necessary to begin by acquiring the tools of that art; and in order that they may be useful it is necessary that they be strong enough to fulfil their function. To learn to think then, it is essential to make use of our limbs, senses and organs, for they are the instruments of our intelligence; and, to extract the fullest use from these instruments, the body which carries them must be robust and healthy. Far from it being true that reason develops independently of the body, it is a good bodily state which makes the operations of the mind easy and sure. (I) 128. (V) 90.

Children require much sleep since they also require a great deal of exercise. The one balances the other so they are in need of both. The time marked out by nature for repose is the night. It is common knowledge that sleep is more tranquil and sweet whilst the sun is below the horizon; when the atmosphere is warmed by its rays our senses are not preserved in such a calm.... But life in society is not so simple and natural, so free of upsets and accidents (as say it is in the country and in a state of nature) that one ought to accustom men to this uniformity to the point that it is vital to them. Without doubt he should submit to rules but the first rule is that he should be capable of infringing the rule without risk if occasion demands. Do not be so lacking in discretion as always to allow your pupil to sleep as long as possible therefore. At the outset do not interfere with the law of nature but do not be unmindful of the fact that, among men, he will have to be above this law; he ought to learn to go to bed late, to rise early, be rudely awakened, and to pass a night unsleeping without being indisposed. Begin quite soon, proceeding gently and by degrees. . . .

I shall sometimes awaken *Émile* less to guard against a habit of sleeping overlong than to accustom him to anything, including being awakened suddenly. Furthermore I should be unfitted for my task if I could not train him to wake of his own accord and rise as I desired without my saying a word to him. If he sleeps too little I shall allow him to contemplate the prospect of a day with a boring morning so that he will count as a gain any time which he gives to sleep; if he sleeps too late I shall show to him at his waking an amusement which is to his liking. When I wish him to awaken at an appointed time I shall tell him that at six o'clock I am going fishing or taking a walk to some spot or other and would he like to go. He consents and requests that I wake him; I promise or do not as the need seems to be. If he wakes too late he finds I have departed. There is something very wrong if he does not soon learn to wake of his own accord. (I) 133/4/5. (V) 94/95.

A sluggish and indolent child was to be trained as a runner although he had no penchant for this exercise or any other despite the fact that he was destined to become a soldier; he was convinced, I know not how, that one of his class required neither to do nor know anything, that the nobility of his birth stood in lieu of arms, legs and for all varieties of virtue. . . . The difficulty was the greater in that I wished to issue no orders at all. I had given up any rights I might have had to preach, promise, threaten, exemplify or display; how was I to get him to run without saying anything? Merely running myself was unlikely to appeal and possessed of many drawbacks.

When walking with him of an afternoon I sometimes took with me in my pocket two cakes of a kind of which he was especially fond; we would each eat one whilst walking and return perfectly content. One day he noticed that I had three cakes and since he was very able to eat six without the slightest trouble he speedily consumed the one I gave him and asked for the third. No, I told him. I could eat it without difficulty myself or we could divide it between us, but I would rather see those two young people race for it. I called them over, showed the cake and made my proposal. They needed no further asking. (I) 150/151. (V) 105/106.

The number of cakes taken on the walk is increased and more competitors enlisted until the event becomes one having considerable spectator value, even for the one child for whom all this is intended as a lesson.

Growing somewhat jaundiced at constantly seeing much coveted cakes consumed under his very eyes the young gentleman began to form the opinion that maybe there was some good in running, and taking note of the fact that he did have two legs, began to practice the business in secret.

I took care to see nothing of this but I knew that my plan was working. When he thought that he was good enough—and I was of the same opinion—he acted as if pleading with me to give him the remaining cake. I refused. He persisted, then with a defiant air, said, 'Very well then, put it on the stone and mark out the course and we shall see.'

'Excellent!' I replied with laughter. 'Does a gentleman propose to race? You will gain a greater appetite but nothing with which to satisfy it.'

Piqued by my derision he made a great effort, carried off the prize with ease because I had made the course short and had ensured that the fastest runner was not present. It goes without saying that after this I had no difficulty in getting him to stay in training. Before long he took such joy in this exercise that, with no inducement, he was sure to vanquish the village lads in a race however long the course was made.

This advantage produced another of which I had not dreamed. When he rarely won the prize he always ate it himself as did his rivals, but when he became accustomed to being victorious he became generous and often shared with the losers. That provided me with a lesson in morals and I learned from it the true principle of generosity. (I) 152. (V) 106.

Just what it is that was learned by the observation of the child's behaviour as a regular victor is not explicitly stated. It is to be presumed that Rousseau wishes to draw attention once more to the statement that it is weakness and inability not strength and power which tends to produce immoral action.

As has already been stressed, Rousseau's main concern at this stage of a child's education is with the use of the senses. He discusses the employment of each of the five senses in turn.

A child is smaller than a man; he possesses neither his strength nor his reason, but he sees and hears as well as a man or very nearly so; his sense of taste is also acute though less discriminating, and he can distinguish one odour from another very well although not with the same sensuality. The first faculties which come to perfection in us are the senses. They are then the first that should be cultivated, yet they are the very ones that people overlook and neglect the most.

To train the senses is not solely a matter of use; it is to learn to make sound judgments by employing them, to learn to be informed by sense so to speak because we neither touch nor see nor hear with any understanding but that we have been taught to do so.

There can be a merely natural and mechanical exercise of the
senses which serves the body and preserves it without adding to
judgment: to swim, run, jump, whip a top, throw stones—all this is
fine, but have we only arms and legs? Have we not also eyes and
ears and are these organs superfluous to the employment of those
others? Do not exercise physical strength alone but all the senses
which guide its employment, making the fullest use of each and verify-
ing the impression gained from one by comparing it with that gained
from another. Measure, weigh and compare. Do not use one's
strength until you have estimated how much strength is required;
always see to it that the estimation of the effect precedes the employment of the means. Arouse in the child an enthusiasm for never
making insufficient or superfluous efforts. If you accustom him to
foresee the effects of all his movements in this way and to redress his
errors from his experience, is it not obvious that the more he does the
more judicious he will become?

Suppose that one intends to move something heavy; if he takes too
long a lever he will waste much of his effort; if he uses one too short
his strength will be insufficient. Experience will teach him to choose
precisely the right length of lever for the job. This understanding is
not impossible to one of our pupil's years. Suppose him to have to
carry a load; if he wants to carry as much as he can bear and no
more than that, must he not estimate the weight by the look of it?
Does he know how to compare masses of the same substance but of
differing quantity and to choose between amounts of the same size
but of differing material? He must apply himself to a study of their
specific weights. I have seen a young man, a very good pupil, who
refused to believe until he had proven it, that a bucket full of large
chips of oak was less weighty than the same bucket filled with water.

We are not the master of all our senses to an equal extent. We are
conscious of the activity of the sense of touch at all times when we
are awake; it is active over the whole surface of the body like a guard
constantly vigilant to warn against what may harm us. It is also the
case, whether we will or not, that we gain experience of it by the
fact of its continual exercise and so have the less need to make
special efforts to acquire use of it. Nevertheless it is observable that
the blind possess a surer and more discriminating sense of touch
than we do because, dispossessed of sight, they must needs draw upon
the former sense for that which is supplied for us by the latter. Why
then are we not trained to find our way in darkness as they are able,
to identify things by touch as we come upon them; in a word, to do
by night and without light all that they can do by day and without
eyes? We have the advantage over them so long as it is day, but in
darkness they become our guides in their turn. We are blind for half
our lives; the difference is that the truly blind always know how to
conduct themselves whilst we dare not do anything at night. You
will tell me that we have lights. Ah! always we have artificial substi-
tutes. Can anyone guarantee that they will always be to hand? For

myself I would far rather that *Émile* had eyes in his finger tips than in the chandler's shop.

Were you to be shut up in a building in the middle of the night then clap your hands; you will perceive from the sound you make if the space is large or small and if you are in the centre of it or in a corner. A half pace from the wall the air is stiller than elsewhere and has a different effect upon your face. Remain in one spot and turn completely around; if there is an open door then a slight current of air will indicate its whereabouts. (I) 137/8/9. 137. 138. 139. (V) 97/98.

When I can hear absolutely nothing I am just as uneasy (as when I can see nothing) because, once more, I may be taken unawares. I must suppose things to be as they were before and so ought still to be, that I see what I do not see. Thus forced to employ my imagination, very soon I am no longer its master and that which I used to reassure myself now only alarms me more. If I hear a noise now I hear robbers; if I hear no noise I see ghosts; the wariness that served self preservation now only makes me the more afraid. My reason ought to reassure me but instinct speaks with the louder voice. Of what good is it to think that there is nothing to fear since then one has nothing to do.

The cause of the trouble indicates the remedy. In all things the familiar quiets the imagination; it is only aroused by that which is novel. . . . The roofer's head does not spin when he is on the housetop, and those accustomed to darkness are not afraid of it (I) 142. (V) 99/100.

What advantages has a man thus trained over other men? His steps are customarily sure in the dark, his hands expertly explore all that he encounters and conduct him safely in the darkest of places. His imagination, enriched by childhood games in the dark, sees things as alarming only with difficulty. (I) 145. (V) 102.

Touch is centred upon the man himself; sight ranges beyond his person, a fact which renders it deceitful; with the flick of an eye a man takes in half of his surroundings. How can this multitude of simultaneous sensations and the judgments they excite, fail to produce errors? Thus sight is, of all our sensations the most faulty, precisely because it has the greatest scope; it is activated before the other senses and its results are too prompt and too extensive to be susceptible to correction by the others. Furthermore the illusions of perspective are essential to us if we are to gain a knowledge of special relationships. Without false appearance we should see nothing as at a distance; without gradations of size and illumination we would be unable to estimate distance; indeed it would not exist for us. If of two trees, the one a hundred paces from us appeared to us to be as large and distinct as the one but ten paces away, we should say that they were side by side. . . .

The only way by which we are able to judge of the size and distance of an object is through knowledge of the angle which it forms in respect of our eye; and as this gap is a simple effect of a composite cause, the judgment produced in us allows each cause to remain undetermined or is necessarily faulty. How can one tell simply by sight if the way in which an object appears as smaller than another is because it is, in fact, smaller or because it is farther away?

It is necessary here to adopt a method opposite to the general rule; instead of simplifying the sensation, conjoin it with another to verify it; subject the eye to the hand and, so to speak, restrain the impetuosity of the first by the ordered regularities of the second. In default of following this practice our estimations are very inexact. We have no precision in a mere glance for judgment of heights, lengths, breadths or distances and the proof that the fault is not in the sense itself but in our employment of it is that engineers, surveyors, architects, brick-layers and painters are generally quicker and more accurate in their estimations than we are because their occupations give them the experience which we fail to acquire; they check the appearance of things against other experiences and so determine the relationship of dual causes of an appearance.

Anything that brings unconstrained movement of the body comes easily to children. There are therefore many ways of interesting them in measuring, noticing and estimating distances. There is a very tall cherry tree; how shall we gather the cherries? Will the ladder in the barn be long enough? There is a very wide stream; how are we going to get across? Will one of the planks in the yard span it from side to side? We would like to fish in the moats of the chateau from our windows; what ought to be the length of our line? I want to make a swing attached to two trees; will a rope twelve feet in length be suffi-cient for this? I'm told that our room in the next house will be twenty five feet square; do you think this will suit? Is it larger than our present room? We are extremely hungry; there are two villages; which of the two can we reach the soonest and so eat? And so on. (I) 149/150. (V) 104/105.

One cannot very well learn to judge of the spatial characteristics of bodies without becoming familiar with their shapes and making imitations of them because the basis for this imitation depends abso-lutely upon the laws of perspective. One cannot very well estimate how something will look without some feeling for these laws.

Children, being great imitators, attempt to draw everything: I would wish my pupil to cultivate this art, not so much for the art itself but to make the eye more true and the hand more dextrous— in general I attach little importance to his knowing this or that exercise, but want him to gain from it clarity of sense impression and good bodily control. I shall be most careful to guard against giving him a drawing master who would only set him to copy copies and draw from drawings; I wish him to have no other master than nature, no other model than the thing itself. I want him to have the original itself before his eyes not its representation upon paper, so that he draws a house from a house, a tree from a tree, a man from a man, thus accustoming himself to accurate observation of the way things appear and to reject false and conventionalised copies. (I) 134. (V) 108.

Furthermore, in this activity as in all others, I do not intend my pupil to amuse himself in solitude. I wish his activity to be made yet more agreeable by constantly entering into it with him. I do not want him to have any other rival than myself but I shall be his rival without cease and without risk—that will add to the interest of his occupation without causing jealousy between us. Following his lead I shall take up a pencil and, at first, I shall use it as clumsily as he does. . . . (In improving upon this) I shall progress at more or less the same rate as he does, or I shall advance by such small degrees of skill that he can always catch me up easily and often do better still ... We shall colour things, we shall paint, we shall daub; but in all our daubings we shall ceaselessly observe nature; all we do will be under the eye of that master.[1]

I have said that geometry is not within the scope of the child but it is our fault. We fail to notice that their way is not ours and that that which, for us, involves the art of reasoning should involve for them the art of seeing. Instead of giving them our way we would be better taking up theirs, because our manner of learning geometry is just as much an affair of imagination as it is reasoning. When the proposition is stated one has to imagine the proof; that is to say one must find what proposition, previously acquired, it is consequent upon and then, of all the possible consequences derivable from that prior proposition, choose just the one that is required.

In this way the most exact of reasoners may find himself out of luck if he is not inventive. What devolves from this? In place of our being required to find the proofs they are dictated to us; instead of our learning to use our reason, to master techniques of reasoning, our memories alone are exercised. Draw exact figures; combine them; superimpose the one upon the other; examine their correspondences; you will discover all of elementary geometry by progressing from one observation to the next without there being any mention of definitions or of problems, with no other form of demonstration than simple superimposition. For myself I do not pretend or claim to teach geometry to Émile; it is he who teaches it to me—I shall search for relationships and he will find them, because the way in which I search will lead him to discover them. For example, instead of using a compass to trace out a circle, I trace it with a pencil at the end of a cord attached to a pivot. After doing that, when I want to compare the radii, Émile laughingly points out that the same cord, fully extended could not give unequal distances from the pivot. (I) 155/156. (V) 109/110.

[1] *Passages such as this were greatly to impress Pestalozzi and to shape his teaching methods.*

By degrees Rousseau suggests that the tutor can pretend to find himself in predicaments of increasing complexity until the use of instruments is discovered and then the same instruments can be produced and used.

> People neglect the exactitude of the figures themselves; they are merely supposed to be exact and the proofs of propositions attached to them. Between us, on the contrary, it is not a matter of proofs; our principal concern is with the drawing of truly straight lines, perfectly correct, as accurate as possible; the perfect square and the absolutely round circle. To verify the accuracy of the figure we will check all its sensible properties and that will provide us with opportunities each day for the discovery of something new. . . . Geometry for my pupil is the art that is best served by the proper use of the rule and the compass; he ought not to confuse it with drawing or he will employ neither of these instruments. (I) 157. (V) 110.

Thus, in the service of sensory training, what is normally a study served by the construction of figures is transmuted into a training in draughtsmanship. However, Rousseau's purpose is served admirably by this somewhat cavalier interpretation of what geometry consists in; the senses of touch and of sight are brought together with peculiar intimacy in an activity rigorously demanding of accuracy of observation and of execution. The judgments involved in the activity are such as may be said to 'spring up at one' from the sensory evidence which presents itself. And all of this is as play to the pupil.

> . . . one ought always to think of all this as being nothing other than play, easy and voluntary actions that their nature asks for, the art of varying their games to make them the more agreeable, without the smallest amount of constraint which would transform them into a labour, for what games do they play which provide me with no opportunity for instructing them? (I) 160. (V) 112.

All of this is consistent with Rousseau's analysis of the faculty of reason as consisting in a compound of the five senses and supposed to develop in accordance with the extent to which the latter are developed.

> What I have said of the two senses whose use is the most continuous and important serves well to indicate the manner of exercising the other senses. Sight and touch have equal application to bodies at rest and bodies in motion, but as it is only the disturbance of air which activates the sense of hearing it is only a body in movement which creates a noise or sound; if all things were still we should hear nothing. At night then, when only we ourselves move as we please, we have nothing to fear but bodies which are moving and

it is important to have an alert ear to be able to judge from the sensations which come to us, if the body which is the cause is large or small, far off or near; if the disturbance is violent or feeble. Once the air is disturbed it is subject to repercussions which reverberate, producing echoes repeating the sensations, and cause us to hear the noise or sound as if emanating from another direction than it actually does. If in a plain or in a valley one puts one's ear to the ground, one can hear the voices of men and the sound of hoofbeats when they are much farther off than if one remains upright.

Just as we have compared what we see with what we touch, it is good to do the same in respect of hearing and to be aware which of the two impressions coming at the same time from the same body arrives the most speedily. When one sees the flash of a cannon one is still able to take cover, but when one hears the explosion there is no time, the missile is upon you.

One is able to judge the distance of a thunderstorm by the interval of time between the flash of lightning and the clap of thunder. Make sure that the child comes to know all these experiences, directly when possible and have him find out the others by induction, but I would far rather that he remained in ignorance of them than that you should tell him about them.

As we have an organ which picks up sound so we have one which makes sound, namely the voice; we have no such reciprocation of organs in respect of sight, and, further, we cannot give back colours as we can sounds. It is a means of cultivating the first sense (hearing) to use the active and the passive organs one with the other. (I) 160/161. (V) 112/113.

Teach your pupil to speak plainly, clearly with good articulation, to pronounce with precision but no affectation, to know and to adopt the appropriate grammatical and poetical accent, to speak so that he can always be heard but not to speak louder than necessary; a fault common among children in school. In all things nothing should be superfluous. (I) 162. (V) 113.

Rousseau now advocates that the child be taught music; even to read music; but once more this is less because of the art itself than because of the sensory training to be gained from conjoining sight with voice and with hearing. In the course of his exposition he contrives to comment upon muddles and ineptitudes of French music teaching and musical notation. Plainly the scant heed paid to his suggestion for a new system of musical notation is not without some sort of revelance to this. This may be why there are some rather curious arguments put forward for the inclusion of the reading of music and the exclusion of the reading of words. However, Rousseau does conclude his disquisition upon music with the words:

But that is enough about music; teach it as you wish provided that it be nothing but play. (I) 164. (V) 115.

After something of a summing up of the stage reached Rousseau now turns to what remains to be done.

We are now well informed concerning the characteristics of bodies other than ourselves, of their weight, their shape, colour, solidity, size, distance, temperature, stability and movement. We are aware of which it is suitable to approach and which to keep at a distance, of the way to overcome their resistance or to preserve ourselves against injury from them but this is not sufficient; our own body is constantly being exhausted and requires constant renewal. (I) 164. (V) 115.

What we see, hear or touch will not meet the case here, and in this way Rousseau contrives to bring in the fourth of the senses.

We should die of hunger or of poisoning if it was necessary to learn from experience the food that would nourish us suitably, but because a supreme bounty provides that which is pleasurable to our senses is also preservative of our being, we are informed as to what is fitting for our stomach by that which is pleasurable to our palate. Man as nature makes him has no other medicine than his own appetite, and, in the primitive state, I have little doubt that the food he found the most agreeable was also the most beneficial for him. (I) 165. (V) 115.

What follows seems to depart somewhat from what we have, by now, become accustomed to expect from Rousseau, namely an outright denunciation of any deviation from the path of the natural. To counterbalance this, however, it is important to remember that Rousseau's thesis is not that the human being should remain in a primitive state but that he should advance in a manner that does not do violence to the natural in him.

There is more. The author of all things provides not only for the needs he gives to us but also for those which we ourselves create in ourselves; and it is to maintain at all times a relationship between our desires and our needs that he allows that our tastes change and alter with our way of life. The more that we distance ourselves from the state of nature the more we lose of our natural tastes; or rather the habits we acquire become a second nature substituted for the original so that none of us retains knowledge of it.
It follows from this that the more natural tastes ought to be the simplest because they are the ones most amenable to transformation; on the other hand when they are whetted and excited by our

whims they take a form which is no longer so flexible. The man who has not yet become fixed in the ways of one country can adjust without distress to the ways of whatever country he may be in; but the man fixed in the ways of one country cannot grow into those of another.

Preserve in the child his primitive tastes for as long as possible; his food should be common and plain that he is not familiarised with sophisticated flavours but do not let him have too restricted a taste.

I am not here discussing whether this manner of life is more healthy or not; it is not this which concerns me. It suffices me to know of my preference that it is in the closest conformity with nature and that it is the one most easily modified to accord with other ways.

Above all, do not give him so fixed a bent that it cannot alter according to need. Do not make it that he will die of hunger in a strange land if he has not a French cook in train nor that he will later think that France is the one country in which the food is fit to eat. What a curious compliment by the way! I would say myself that the French are the only people who do not know what good food is as such; since they require such particular skill to make their dishes eatable.

Of our different senses that of taste is the one which generally affects us the most. For this reason it is the more in our interests to judge accurately which substances we ought to absorb into ourselves than of those things which will merely surround us. A great many things are unremarkable when touched, heard or seen but there is hardly anything which lacks distinctiveness to the taste.

Furthermore the activity of this sense is entirely physical and material; it alone says nothing to the imagination or at least owes less to it than any other sensations where imitation and imagination introduce moral considerations.

Thus, as a general rule, tender and voluptuous hearts, passionate and truly sensitive characters, easily moved by other senses, remain indifferent to this one. From all this, which might seem to rank taste as inferior to the other senses and our inclination towards it the more unworthy, I conclude, on the contrary, that the most suitable of ways to direct children is to lead them by their mouths.

The motive of gluttony is infinitely preferable to that of vanity in that the first is a natural appetite, an immediate outcome of sense, and the second is an outcome of opinion subject to the fancies of men and to all manner of abuse. Gluttony is a childish passion; one which pales before any other; at the least competition it disappears. Oh! believe me the child will only too soon cease to bother about food; and when his heart is too engaged his palate will be but little occupied. When he is grown up a thousand impulsive passions diminish his gluttony but stimulate his vanity because this last passion is the only one which is parasitic upon others and in the end it swallows all. (I) 165/6/7. (V) 116/117.

This is a remarkable passage which cannot be left without some comment. It contains one of the more blatant of Rousseau's perversities of argument. The use of the term 'voluptuous', for example, has direct connection with sensuousness yet is used in a way which appears to remove considerations of sense activities from it. Much more importantly, however, the term 'gluttony' (*gourmandise*) is a term of moral disapprobation. It is difficult to understand therefore just how Rousseau can make employment of it in a context where he is attempting to establish that unimpeded and natural growth cannot be adjudged as other than good, and has previously argued that the use of moral judgments in respect of the child of the age here being considered is quite illegitimate. That the term *is* used to stand for something that is not unreservedly admirable is plain from Rousseau's assurance to us that, provided we let well alone, the child's penchant for eating just as much as he possibly can will be dissipated with growth. That he is somewhat uneasy about this supposed inevitability is plain as the passage continues, for we are presented with a picture of the grown man who thinks of nothing above food, as no more than a child of forty years old! It would be odd to suggest that a child can see, hear or touch too much; it is inconveniently true that both child and man *can* eat too much. This is the source of Rousseau's problem, and we begin to see why he earlier stated that he was not concerned with matters of health. One is dangerously near to finding that the activation of natural appetites and the operation of at least one sense can be a detriment to the development of the human being unless some kind of constraint is applied.

The argument becomes increasingly paradoxical and complicated from this point, and it would be something of an extravagance to produce it in its entirety here. At one point, and following a very considerable quote from Plutarch, Rousseau writes:

> Although this quotation is irrelevant to my subject I have been unable to resist the temptation to include it, and I believe that few of my readers will hold it against me. (I) 171. (V) 120.

Plutarch is concerned, in the passage quoted, with the morality of killing other living creatures in order to eat them. Prior to that Rousseau had spent some time discussing the state of primitive man when conditions were such that he went hungry. There are obvious problems for him in both these considerations. Morality is involved in the first, the general beneficence of a state of nature in the second. Finally, and without any real progression which must necessitate our agreement, he arrives at the conclusion:

> ... whatever sort of regimen you bring to children attend to it that they are only accustomed to common and simple fare; let them eat, run and play as they please and you can be certain that they will never eat too much nor have indigestion.
> Our appetite is only immoderate because we wish to regulate by rules other than that of nature ... (I) 171. (V) 120.

If gluttony is the outcome of a natural appetite one wonders how it is that the rule of nature can eliminate it.

There would seem to be a confusion in Rousseau's thinking between appetite and the sense of taste which has something of the same characteristics as the confusion between language and speech which has earlier been commented upon.

The last of the senses to be considered is that of smell.

> The sense of smell is to the sense of taste as the sense of sight is to the sense of touch; it precedes it, it informs it that such and such a substance ought to affect it and whether that substance is to be sought after or avoided.

> Smells of themselves are feeble sensations; they influence the imagination more than the senses and affect one not so much by what they themselves provide but by what they indicate may be looked forward to. (I) 172. (V) 121.

> Smell is the sense of the imagination; giving the nerves a strong tone it must have great activation in the brain; it is for this reason that it revives the character momentarily but exhausts it in the long run.

> The sense of smell ought not then to be very active in the early years. The imagination is as yet little animated by passions and so not greatly susceptible to emotion; nor has one had sufficient experience to anticipate from one sense that which is promised from another. (I) 173. (V) 121.

Nevertheless, some experience of smell is deemed necessary; namely that which connects the sense of smell with that of taste through the imagination. A child should be able accurately to forecast what food is prepared for him by what smells reach him before he either sees or tastes the food. And with the increasing importance of the role of imagination this stage of childhood is all but at an end. Properly fostered in the growth and development of his senses, the child is ready to progress.

His face, his bearing and his looks announce assurance and contentment; health glows in his countenance; his firm step lends him a vigorous air; his colour, delicate but not insipid, has nothing effeminate about it; air and sun have already put the honourable stamp of manliness upon him; his well rounded muscles already bespeak a budding physique; his eyes, that the flame of feeling has not yet illuminated, have, at least all their natural serenity ... (I) 176/177. (V) 124.

Make him a place in the middle of the assembly: examine him, gentlemen; interrogate him in all confidence; have no fear that he will be troublesome or prattle or ask indiscreet questions. Do not fear that he will overbear you or expect you to dance constant attendance upon him or that you will be unable to get away from him. Do not expect pretty words from him either, nor that he will merely say what I have told him to say; expect nothing but the truth, plain and simple, without elaboration, affectation or vanity. He will tell you of the wrong things he has done and thought with just the same freedom as he tells of the good; without embarrassment about the effect of what he says upon you. . . .

His ideas are limited but clear; he knows nothing by heart but much by experience; if he reads our books less well than other children he reads that of nature very much better; his spirit is not in his tongue but in his head; his judgment is greater than his memory; he only speaks the one language but he knows what he says, and if his speech is less fluent than other children's this is counterbalanced by the fact that his deeds are better. (I) 177/178. (V) 124/125.

He knows nothing that is mere routine, customary, or habitual; that which he does today has little influence on that which he will do tomorrow; he follows no formula and concedes to no authority or pattern; he speaks and acts as it occurs to him to do. . . .

You will find he has but few moral notions but all bear a direct relationship to his actual state and not the state of a grown man, for how would these serve him when he is not yet an active member of society? Speak to him of freedom, property and even of convention. He may understand you thus far. He knows why that which is his is his and that which is not his is not; beyond that he knows nothing. Speak to him of duty, obedience and he will not know what you are talking about; command him to do something and he will not listen to you, but say to him, 'If you will do me this kindness I will do the same in return' and instantly he will endeavour to please you.

On his own account, if he is in need of some assistance he will ask it of the first person he encounters without regard as to identity; he would ask the king as soon as he would ask his lackey; all men are

equal in his eyes. You will see from the manner of his asking that
he is aware you owe him nothing; he knows that he asks a favour.

He has attained the fullness of childhood; he has lived the life of a
child and has not paid for his progress with his happiness.

The great inconvenience of this early education is that what it is
is only discernible by far sighted people; to the uninformed eye this so
carefully brought up child appears to be a mere scamp. (I) 178/9/
180/181. (V) 125/126/127.

With this first record of educational attainment the second phase
of childhood is at an end.

D

Chapter Three

DAWNINGS OF INTELLECT

At this point in *Émile*; namely at the age of twelve or thirteen, Rousseau considers the emergence of the faculty of reason. Still having no truck with the established practices, the tutor is now concerned with facilitating the development of this faculty in a pupil even more difficult to call a child than it was to call the child of the second book an infant.

> Until the time of adolescence the whole course of a life is a time of weakness but it is at a point in this first stage that strength develops beyond the demands of need; the growing creature, yet absolutely weak, is nevertheless relatively strong. His needs are not fully developed, the powers which he has are more than sufficient to meet them. As a man he would be very weak, as a child he is very strong.
>
> What is the source of the weakness of men? It is the inequality which is to be found between their powers and their desires. Our passions make us weak because to satisfy them requires more power than nature gave us. Diminish these desires then and it is as if you add to your strength; he who is able to do more than he desires has strength to spare; this is to be really strong. Now is the third stage of childhood and that of which I have now to speak. I continue to talk of childhood for want of a better word; by this age the child is approaching adolescence without yet having reached puberty.
>
> At twelve or thirteen the powers of the child develop much more rapidly than his needs. The more violent and terrible of passions is as yet unknown to him; the organ (of sex) remains incompletely developed and seems to await the command of the will. (I) 182. (V) 128.

Rousseau thus continues with the testimonial commenced at the conclusion to the second book of *Émile*. Immune to climatic changes, with no epicurean appetites artificially inspired, content to sleep wherever he finds himself when tired, unaffected by any artificially titivated longings beyond his realisation, independent of the opinion of others; the child is self-sufficient. His competence more than suffices to meet his plans.

> How then should he use this reserve of ability and power which is greater than what is requisite to him for his present needs and which will never be his again? Why, he employs what he has to meet those needs, then, as it were, banks the surplus against what is to come; the robust child makes provision for the feeble man, but he sets up his store where it cannot be stolen, not in barns open to strangers but in places peculiarly his own; in his arms, his head—it is lodged within himself. Now, therefore, is the time for work, instruction and study; and take note that this is no arbitrary choice of mine; it is nature herself which indicates it. (I) 183. (V) 129.

This passage contains the keynote to the procedures to be followed by the tutor. These will differ somewhat from the stage of growth immediately preceding this one. The move is out of the so-called 'negative education' which has previously been advocated.

> Human intelligence is finite; no man is able to know everything or even to gain all the scanty sum of knowledge other men have. Since the contradictory to every false proposition is the truth, the number of truths is as inexhaustible as the number of falsehoods. We have a choice to make as to what to teach and when to teach it. Of that which is within our comprehension some things are false, others useless; others again only serve to nourish arrogance. The little number of things which actually contribute to our well being is alone worthy of the researches of a wise man and, consequently, of a child one wishes to make wise. The question is not what there is to know but simply what it is useful to know. Of this small number of truths one must remove those which demand for their comprehension a fully developed mind; those which suppose an understanding of human relationships which a child is incapable of acquiring; those which, though true in themselves, dispose an inexperienced intellect to false beliefs on other subjects.
>
> Remember; remember always, that ignorance does no one harm; error alone is deadly. We are not misled by what we do not know but by what we believe we do know. (I) 184. (V) 129.

> A single instinct activates the diverse abilities of men. The activity which seeks the development of the body is succeeded by the activity which seeks to instruct the mind. At first sight children appear merely restless, then they become curious, and this governing curiosity is the moving force of our attainments. Always distinguish between the inclinations inspired by nature and those stemmed from opinion. He is an avid searcher for the knowledge which is worth knowing; this is no wish merely to appear learned but a curiosity natural to

man in respect of all things both near and far, which may affect him. The inborn desire for well-being, and the impossibility of completely satisfying it, leads him to search ceaselessly for new means of contributing towards it. Such is the first principle of curiosity; one natural to the human heart though the extent of its development is dependent upon our passions and our understandings. (I) 185. (V) 129.

Reject from our first studies therefore the knowledge which possesses no natural attraction for us, and limit ourselves to that which instinct urges us to find.

The earth is humanity's island; the most impressive object which our eyes behold is the sun. Just as soon as we begin to look beyond ourselves our observations must be of the one or the other. Thus it is that the philosophising of almost all primitive peoples all but completely consists in imaginary divisions of the earth and in stating the divine characteristics of the sun.

What a deviation from what has been so far put forward, you will say. Constantly till now we have been occupied with what touches us, with our immediate surroundings; all of a sudden here we are, surveying the globe and reaching out to the extremities of the universe! The change is the consequence of the increase of our powers and the impulsions of our spirit. In the state of feebleness and insufficiency our care centred upon our own preservation. In the state of increased efficacy and power the desire to extend ourselves carries us beyond ourselves and as far beyond as possible; but, since the world of ideas is as yet unknown to us, our thoughts are limited by our vision and our understanding can only grow to that extent.

Let our sensations be transformed into ideas but not leap all at once from the sensible to the abstract; it is by the first that we eventually acquire the latter. In the first operations of the mind the senses should always be the guide; no other book than the world; no other teaching than the facts. The child who reads does not think but only reads; he is merely gaining words not knowledge.

Make sure your pupil is attentive to the phenomena of nature; he will very soon be curious; to nourish this curiosity do not hasten to satisfy it however. Acquaint him with the questions; have him resolve them for himself. He should know nothing because you have told him but because he has understood it himself. He should not be taught science; he should discover it. If ever you substitute authority for reason in his mind he will reason no more; he will become the toy of others opinions. (I) 186. (V) 130/131.

Always bear in mind that the essential of my method is not to teach the child a great many things but never to allow anything into his head but exact and clear ideas. That he knows nothing is of little importance to me provided that he is not mistaken, and I only put truths in his head which will guarantee that error will not take their place. Reason and judgment come to us slowly, but prejudices rush upon us in crowds; it is from them that he must be preserved. But if you consider science in itself you embark upon a bottomless sea, without shores and abounding in hazards; you will never extricate yourself from it. When I see a man in love with knowledge and allowing himself to be seduced by its lures; carried from one thing to another unable to stop, I believe I see a child on the sea shore gathering shells, first loading himself, then, tempted by others he now sees, jettisoning those he has, then recovering them again until he is so overburdened that he abandons all and returns with nothing. (I) 191. (V) 134.

Bear in mind that the passions approach him and that, as soon as they knock at the door, your pupil will have no attention for anything else. The peaceful time of intelligence is so short, it passes so swiftly and so much use of it is necessary that it is folly to utilise it to make a child learned. It is not your task to teach him the sciences but to give him the liking for them that will lead him to acquire their methods once this taste has matured. This is undoubtedly a fundamental principle of all good education.

If he questions you himself, reply in such a way as to nourish his curiosity but not to satisfy it; however when you see that instead of questioning you in order to be instructed he is merely casting about and overwhelming you with silly queries, immediately cease to respond, for it is evident that he no longer cares about things but wishes solely to enslave you by his interrogation. One must have less regard for the words he utters than for the motive which prompts him to speak. Before this time this warning was hardly apposite but it becomes supremely important immediately the child begins to reason. (I) 192. (V) 135.

To the extent that the child advances in intelligence other important considerations oblige us to be increasingly careful in the choice of his occupations. As soon as he has sufficient understanding of himself to know what contributes to his well being; as soon as he is able to apprehend the wide ranging relationships necessary to judge that which is to his benefit and that which is not, then he is at a point when he can distinguish between work and play and to look upon the latter only as a means of refreshing oneself for the other. This being so, subject matter of real utility may be introduced into his studies and so engage him that he gives to them more persistence of attention than he once gave to his games. (I) 200. (V) 140.

It is to be noticed that Rousseau is now accrediting his pupil with the ability to conceptualise his activities as either serious or non-serious; that is to say, to make value judgments about the worth of what he is doing. It is also clear that it is now permissible to introduce the child to specific activities, even though the manner of so doing is severely delimited.

The 'growth model' of education is also very apparent now. Reason, it appears, is growing. It must be nurtured, appropriately fed and allowed to unfold according to the pre-ordained pattern of the natural. Questions are important now, both of the child and from him, but there are questions and questions. Some spring from natural promptings, others from other sources.

From the time that they can anticipate their needs before they feel them, their intelligence is greatly advanced; they begin to value time. It is of moment from this point that they are trained to employ time in the pursuit of useful ends but of a usefulness appropriate to their age and that is within the reach of their comprehension. All that touches upon the moral order and the ways of society should not be presented to them as yet for they are not yet capable of under-standing it. It is inept to expect of them an attention to things which are vaguely explained as for their good at an age when they do not comprehend what it is for something to be good, and then to assure them that these things will profit them when grown up. They have no present interest in this pretended profit. They do not understand.

The child should do nothing by command; nothing is to his good that he does not himself see as such. In constantly flinging things at him which are beyond his understanding, you believe you are bring-ing foresight into play, yet, in fact, it is foresight that you lack. To provide him with ineffectual instruments which he may never employ you deprive him of the most useful of tools—that of good sense; you bring him to allow himself always to be led, to be nothing but a machine in the hands of others. You would have him docile when a child; this is to wish him to be a credulous fool when grown. You say to him time and again; 'All that I ask of you is to your advantage but you are not yet able to understand this. Of what importance is it to me that you do not do these things? It is solely for your own benefit that you work.' With all these fine speeches that you make to him now to bring him wisdom you prepare a road to success for the dreamer, the windbag, the charlatan, the knave and all species of fool who will set traps for him and draw him into folly. (I) 200/201. (V) 141.

As soon as we succeed in giving our pupil an idea of the word 'use-ful' we have gained a great new way of controlling him; for this word has much significance, given that it has, for him, a sense appropriate to his age and that he sees clearly how it relates to his own well-being. Generally children are not impressed with the word because you take no care to convey an idea within their comprehension and because others always undertake for them that which is useful for them so they have no need to think for themselves and do not know what to be useful can mean.

Whatever good is that? Henceforth this is the sacred watchword, the controlling question by which both he and I order all the actions of our lives; this is the question with which I invariably counter all his questions and which serves to check the incessant stream of stupid and finicky interrogations with which children fatigue everyone without point; questions asked more to exercise control over people than to gain profit. From this they are taught a most important lesson; they learn to seek nothing that has not utility; to inquire after the manner of Socrates who never asked a question without a purpose, for now the child realises that he will be asked for his reason before his question is answered.

Consider what a powerful instrument I have placed into your hands with which to affect your pupil. He knows the reason for nothing; you can all but reduce him to silence whenever you please, and, conversely, what advantage is lent to your knowledge and experience as you seek to show him the usefulness of all that you propose to him! Make no mistake, to put this question to him is to teach him to put it to you in his turn. You can count on it that of all that you propose to him he will copy your example and say; 'Whatever good is that?'

Here we come across what is perhaps the most difficult trap for a tutor to avoid. If upon the child's questioning you like this, you weary of the affair and give him a single reason which he cannot understand, seeing that you reason by ideas suitable for you and not by his own, he will believe that what you tell him is good for your age of person and not for his own; he will place no more faith in you and all is lost. But where is the master who would wish to stop short and talk over his faults with his pupil? All of us make it a rule never to own the faults that, in fact, we have; yet I would make it a duty to admit even to faults I have not when I found myself unable to make my reasons understood by him; thus my conduct would always be clearly apprehended and he would harbour no suspicions of me. I should gain more credit by supposing faults I have not than those who conceal those they have.

Firstly, keep firmly in mind that it is rarely your duty to propose to him that which he ought to learn; it is for him to want to learn, to search and to find; for you to put things in his way, to awaken that desire adroitly and to furnish the means for its satisfaction. (I) 202/203. (V) 142.

By this time it is becoming increasingly evident that Rousseau is advancing his argument that the faculty of reason, this 'sixth sense' compounded out of impressions received from the other five, is to be the essential interest of the tutor. He now goes a step further. Much has been said previously about the necessity to allow freedom of *movement*, and this has been associated with the notion of 'activity'. In the following passage, and in respect of the age of child now under consideration, it becomes clear that Rousseau has no limited notion of what an activity can be. It is not restricted to bodily engagements. These are to be unconstrained as before of course, but the emphasis is explicitly stated as being upon the activities of observation, examination and judgment. It is the development of these that the tutor is watchful over.

> Reader, do not delay yourself to watch the bodily movements and manual dexterity of your pupil, but think what direction we are giving to his childish curiosity; think of his common sense, his inventive mind and his foresight; consider the head he will have. He will want to gain familiarity with everything he sees and does; he will want to know the reason for everything.... He will go back to first principles, he will take nothing for granted; he will refuse to learn anything that demands prior knowledge which he does not possess. (I) 216. (V) 151.

Plainly this can be an exciting time for the tutor, but this fact contains a certain danger which must be guarded against.

> However, one fault difficult to avoid in activities which passionately interest the master, is to suppose, of necessity, the same degree of interest in the child; be careful that you are not swept on by your own interest in the work whilst the child is bored with it although he does not dare to let you see this. The child must be completely absorbed in his activity but you must be absorbed in the child; you must watch him; you must watch him without relaxing vigilance yet without it being obvious to him.
> Anticipate all his feelings that you may prevent him having undesirable ones; occupy him in such a way that not only does he think himself usefully employed but he finds pleasure in the employment from really understanding the value of what he is doing. (I) 217. (V) 151.

Building upon this, Rousseau is now able to introduce considerations of a general nature, which, it will become plain later on, are inspired by the work which *Émile* was intended to accompany, namely *The Social Contract*.

> No society can exist without trade; no trading without a commonly accepted standard; no such standard without equality. Thus, for its law, each society has some conventional equality, be it in men or things.
> The conventional equality between men, (very different from natural equality) makes positive right necessary, that is to say government and law. The political understanding of a child must be clear and limited; he must know of government in general that which concerns the right of ownership, of which he already has some idea.
> Conventional equality between things caused currency to be invented, for currency is only a term of comparison for the evaluation

of different kinds of things. In this sense money is the true bond of the society; once it was in beasts; shells are still used by several races; in Sparta it was iron, in Sweden, leather; we use gold and silver. Metals, being easier to carry about, have generally been the commonest form of currency. One has converted these metals into money to avoid constant weighing and measuring at each exchange, for the denomination of each coin is only an attestation that the piece thus marked is of a certain weight. The sovereign alone has the right to mint coin since he alone can demand recognition of his authority by the people. (I) 218. (V) 152.

Rousseau then states that the most stupid of persons can comprehend the way in which money acts intermediately between commodities where there is no real basis of comparison, say between cloth and corn. The convention is a necessary one. Goods can now be given comparative values.

Go no farther than this with your pupil and do not enter into an explanation of the moral effects of this institution. In everything it is important to make clear the uses before showing the abuses. If you mean to explain to children how tokens lead one to neglect things, how money gives rise to all the chimeras of opinion, how countries which are rich in silver must be poor in everything else, you will be treating children not only as philosophers but as wise men, and you will be claiming to teach them what few philosophers have understood themselves. On what a wealth of interesting objects one is able to turn the curiosity of a pupil without ever leaving the relationship with the real and the material which is within his grasp, therefore never admit into a pupil's mind a single idea that is not within his understanding. The art of the master consists in his ability to make all his pupil's observations of significance. The child should know nothing of the trifling but constantly advance towards the important relations that, in time, he ought to know in order to judge well that which is good and that which is bad in a society. Tutors must know how to turn an amusing conversation to the advancement of the mind of the pupil. Questions which do not even graze the attention of others will torment Émile for six months. (I) 219. (V) 153.

... my method is independent of my examples; it is based upon the measure of man's faculties at different stages of his growth and on the choice of activities which are in accord with them. I believe that one could easily find another method which apparently gave better results, but, if it was less appropriate to the nature of the child, to age and to sex, I doubt that it could bring the same success. At the commencement of his second period we have profited by the superabundance of our powers over our needs in being taken beyond ourselves; we have projected ourselves out into the heavens; we have measured the earth; we have catalogued the laws of nature; in a word we have surveyed our entire environment. Now we must return to ourselves; we should gradually reconcile all this with our own habitation.[1] Happy indeed are we, if, upon our return, we do not find in occupation the enemy who menaces us, and who has been preparing to seize it. (I) 222. (V) 155.

Presumably, by the last quoted sentence, Rousseau wishes to refer to the insidious influences of custom and fashion which lead to the enslavement and corruption of man.

What is there left to be done after we have observed all that there is about us? We must convert to our use all that we have been able to gather to ourselves and begin to draw upon our curiosity for the betterment of our well-being. Up till now we have made provision of instruments of all kinds without knowing which ones we need. Perhaps those which are useless for us will prove useful to others; perhaps, in our turn, we shall have need of theirs. Thus we find that exchange is of benefit to all, but for this to be possible we have to know our mutual needs. Each must be aware of what is useful to the other and what he is able to offer in return. If you suppose ten men you must suppose ten different sets of need. To provide for these needs each must apply himself to ten varieties of work, but, according to aptitude and talent, the one who succeeds less at one sort of occupation, the other at another. All of them, fitted for different things but working at all, will be badly served. Form a society of these ten men, letting each work at that for which he is most fitted, both for his own benefit and for that of the other nine, each then profits from the talents of the others as if they were all his own; each perfects his particular care by continual practice and so it turns out for each that, himself well provided for, he has yet plenty to spare for the others. Clearly this is the principle underlying all our institutions. It is not my present concern to comment on how it has worked out; I have done this in another book.[2]

By this argument a man wishing to regard himself in isolation, taking nothing from anyone else, self-sufficient, could be nothing but miserable. It would not even be possible for him to stay alive, because, finding the earth to be entirely partitioned into what is yours and what mine, and having nothing of his own but his body, from whence will he derive what is necessary to him? Upon leaving the state of nature we force our fellows to do so also. No one may

---

[1] '... nous nous rapprochons insensiblement de notre habitation.' *This could be translated otherwise than as above, e.g. It may be said that we should do what is recommended 'unconsciously', but it is difficult to see how this ties in with the import of the whole paragraph and the argument in general.*

[2] *Again* 'Il ne'st pas mon sujet d'en examiner ici les conséquences:' *may be somewhat differently interpreted but it is to be borne in mind that the other book mentioned is the second discourse. (See Introduction.)*

remain in it in defiance of the others. To attempt to do so is only to leave it, for the first law of nature is the preservation of oneself. Thus the idea of social relationships forms itself little by little in the child's mind even before he can actually be an active member of society. Émile comes to see that to have instruments for his use supposes that others have some for their use, for then he is able to exchange things to obtain what is necessary to him and possessed by others. I can easily bring him to realise the need for these exchanges and to profit from the situation. (I) 223/224. (V) 156/157.

As soon as Émile knows what it is to be alive my first care will be to teach him to maintain his life. Up till now I have made no distinctions of state, rank or fortune and I shall continue to guard against so doing because man is the same in all his states; the rich man has a stomach no larger than the poor man and his digestion is no better; the master has an arm no longer or stronger than that of his slave; the great man has a stature no taller than a common man; in the last analysis the natural needs are the same for all. Educate the man as a man and not as what is not part of him. Do you not see that, in working to fit him exclusively for one station in life, you make him unfit for everything else and that, at a turn of fortune, your work can make him wretched? What could be more ridiculous than a great gentleman brought down to destitution, who carries with him into his misery all the prejudices of his birth? What could be more worthless than a once rich man, now impoverished, who reminds himself of the contempt he felt for the poor and so feels himself the lowest of the low? The one may descend to the business of tricking the public; the other to that of a creeping servant with the parrot cry 'I have to live'.

You rely upon the social order as it now is without thinking that this order is subject to inevitable and startling changes[1] which are impossible for you to foresee any more than it is possible to prevent your children from being witness to them. The great become the small, the rich become the poor, the sovereign becomes the subject: are blows of this sort so rare than one can ever count oneself exempt from them? We approach a state of crisis and a century of revolutions. (I) 223/224. (V) 156/157.

To this last sentence Rousseau adds a footnote:

I hold it to be impossible that the great monarchies of Europe can endure for much longer; all are brilliant and all things in such a state must then decline. I have my own opinion as to the more particular reasons to be attached to this general principle but do not propose to speak of them; anyone can see them well enough.

[1] *The original reads '... est sujet à des révolutions inévitables'. The word* 'révolution' *is avoided in the translation simply because the extent to which Rousseau either envisaged or referred to a coming (French) revolution or was pleading for a political upheaval in this context, is a matter of considerable speculation.*

The passage itself continues:

> Who can answer what may befall you? All that is made by man
> may be destroyed by man; the only ineffaceable characters are those
> imprinted by nature and nature makes neither princes nor rich men
> nor great gentlemen. Reduced to a lowly station what will become
> of the petty despot you have educated for grandeur? What will
> happen to the financier in poverty who has known only what it is
> to eat from gold? Deprived of everything what will happen to this
> fastidious imbecile who is capable of nothing himself and takes to be
> his that which, in fact, is not of his making or doing? Under such
> conditions happy is the man who can let fall from him all that can
> fall from him, and remain a man in the face of all adversity.

> The man and the citizen, whoever he may be, has no other thing of
> value to contribute to society than himself; all his other goods are
> independent of him, and when a man is rich he does not enjoy his
> wealth unless the society enjoys it also. In the first case he robs
> others by depriving them; in the second he gives them nothing. Thus
> the debt he owes society is unpaid whilst he renders up only material
> goods. (I) 225/226. (V) 157/158.

> Outside society the man in isolation owes nothing to anyone and
> has a right to live as he pleases; but within society, where the
> necessities of life stem from other people, he owes them in work the
> price of his maintenance. There is no exception to this. Work then is
> an indispensable duty of the man in society. Rich or poor, strong or
> weak, every idle citizen is a thief.
> Now, of all the occupations capable of furnishing a man with
> subsistence, that which most corresponds with the state of nature is
> work with the hands; of all conditions the one most independent of
> fortune and of men is that of the artisan. The artisan only depends
> upon his work; he is free whereas the ploughman is a slave; the
> latter must have his field, the yield of which is at the mercy of others.
> An enemy, a ruler, a powerful neighbour may seize his field; in a
> thousand ways this field may worry him; but whoever might wish to
> vex the artisan, his baggage is quickly packed; he takes his skills and
> is away. (I) 226. (V) 159.

> A trade for my son! 'My son an artisan!' 'Sir, what are you think-
> ing of?' I think better than you do, Madam, who wish to limit him
> to be nothing but a lord, marquis or prince and yet it could be that,
> one day, he may be less than nothing: I wish to give him a rank that
> he can never lose, that will be of honour at any time; I wish to ele-
> vate him to the status of a man and, whatever you may say, fewer
> will equal him in that standing than the many who would were he
> to take yours. The letter kills and the spirit gives life. The question is
> less one of learning a trade for the sake of the trade than to eradicate

the prejudices which are to be despised. You will never be reduced to working for your living? Oh so much the worse; so much the worse for *you*! But never mind; don't work because it is necessary; do so out of pride. Abase yourself to the position of an artisan—in order to be above your own. For you to dominate fortune and circumstance begin by making yourself independent. In order to gain sway by popular opinion begin by freeing yourself of its influence.

Remember that it is not some rare gift or ability that I ask of you; it is a trade, a true trade, a purely mechanical skill by which the hands work more than the head, which does not lead to fortune but which enables you to ignore her. (I) 227. (V) 159.

At this point one may be tempted to wonder whether all this is quite consistent with the general line of the argument. Is to acquire a trade in these conditions and for these reasons in accord with the urging that one should learn nothing that is not essentially useful to the learner? Does it not smack of a 'rainy day' outlook? From what follows it seems not—other things might suffice to provide for the 'rainy day' at least to some extent; that is to say unless complete material disaster befalls the family or individual. However, Rousseau insists upon the consideration of the severest of misfortunes, and one cannot but help recall his own experiences and wonder whether there is not a considerable colouration of the argument by this.

In some houses far above the danger of want of bread I have seen some fathers carry precaution to such a point as to take care that their children are instructed in that which, in any circumstance, would enable them to make a living. These farsighted fathers believe that they are doing something that is very wise; it is nothing because the resources with which they think they have equipped their children depend upon the very fortune above which they are supposed to allow them to rise, so that with all these fine talents, if he who has them does not find himself in favourable circumstances for their employment he perishes in want as if he had none. When it is a question of stratagems and intrigues, employ them to maintain oneself in abundance rather than as the means whereby you may regain, from the depth of poverty, your previous estate. If you cultivate the arts of which the success hangs upon the reputation of the artist, if you prepare yourself for employments only to be obtained by favour, how will all that serve you when, rightly disgusted with the world, you disdain the means without which you are unable to climb?

You have studied politics and the interests of princes. That is all very well but what use have you for these understandings if you have no access to ministers, to the ladies of the court, to the heads of departments, if you have not the secret of gaining their pleasure, if none of them find you to be the rascal to suit their convenience. You are an architect or a painter; well and good, but you must make your talent known. Do you think you can exhibit your work in a salon without any prior arrangement? Oh; it is not done in that way! One has to belong to the Academy; to be somebody's protegé to obtain even the most obscure corner of a wall. Leave aside rule and pencil,[1] take a cab and hasten from door to door; this is the way to acquire recognition. Now you are bound to know that these illustrious portals are opened to you by door keepers who only understand actions and whose ears are in their hands. Do you wish to teach that which you have learned and to become a master of geography, mathematics, languages, music or draughtsmanship? To do even that one must gather scholars as a consequence of people's praises. Count it more important to be a quick witted charlatan and that, if you know nothing but your profession, you know nothing at all. See then that all these brilliant resources are without substance, and how many other resources are necessary if you are to profit from them. (I) 227. (V) 159.

But if, instead of resorting to these rarified understandings as a means of making a living, ones which nourish the head and not the body, you can resort at need to the use of your hands in the practice of a skill, all these problems disappear, all these tricks and stratagems become useless; one's resources are at hand when required; integrity and honour are no longer obstacles to making a living. There is no more need to be faint hearted or to be deceitful before the great, to be pliable and self abasing before rogues, vilely fawning before all, a cadger or thief. The opinion of others does not affect you; you do not have to dance attendance upon anyone, to flatter a fool, to soften up doormen, curry favour with courtesans by showering them with compliments. That the rascally manage the affairs of state is of little moment to you: you are not impeded, you in your humble way of life, able to be honest and to eat. You are able to walk into the first workshop engaged in your trade and say, 'Master, I have need of work.' He replies, 'Journeyman, take a place and get to work.' Before the dinner hour arrives you have earned your dinner; if you are diligent and sober, before the week has passed you have the means to live for another week and you would have lived that first week in freedom, health, truth, industry and uprightness. He does not lose his time who has gained all this.

I am adamant that Émile shall learn a trade. 'But an honest trade,' you may wish to say. What is to be meant by this word 'honest'? Are not all trades that are useful to people honest? I would not wish him to be an embellisher or gilder or varnisher as Locke's pupil was; nor to be a musician, actor or writer of books. With the

---

[1] *In the original there is a shift at this point. Where one read* 'pensez-vous ...' *previously, this sentence commences* 'Quittez-moi la règle ...' *This may indicate the measure of personal involvement in this passage.*

exception of these occupations and others of the same kind let him take on what he wishes; I don't mean to restrain him at all.[1] (I) 229. (V) 160.

Rousseau continues the discussion, but one thing becomes increasingly noticeable, namely that what is happening here is more and more in the nature of a dialogue with himself. A certain informality of style and vagueness of direction characterises this. It is as if he was looking over what he has just said and wondering whether there were not a few amendments to be made.

I would far rather that he was a shoemaker than a poet; far rather that he paved the important roads than painted flowers on porcelain. 'But,' you might protest, 'policemen, spies, executioners—these are useful folk.' If it were not for the government they would be of no use.[2] But let that pass: I am wrong; it is insufficient that the trade chosen be useful; it must also be such that it does not require of people the exercise of qualities of mind which are odious and incompatible with humanity. Thus, to return to the first point, take a trade which is honest but bear in mind always that there is no honesty without usefulness. (I) 229. (V) 160.

It is now clear that the reason for pleading that the pupil learns a trade is essentially based upon moral considerations. Secondly, it is clear that the whole discussion is almost a reiteration of the thesis of the second discourse; that the sciences and arts of men corrupt rather than improve the morals of men.

This is the cast of mind which ought to guide us in our choice of trade for Émile, or rather his choice, for it is he who should do the choosing, not us. The maxims he has acquired have conserved in him a natural contempt for useless things. Never will he wish to occupy his time in work of no value and he attaches value only to the truly useful. For him it must be such a trade as would serve a Robinson Crusoe upon his island. In placing in front of the child a survey of the outcomes of nature and of art one excites his curiosity, one follows where it leads and so has opportunity to study his likes, his inclinations, his aptitudes and to spot with ease the first intimations of his particular gifts if these take some definite direction. But one must preserve oneself from making one common error; it is to attri-

[1] *A footnote to this passage clearly reveals the degree of self-involvement which has now crept in. An imaginary reader challenges Rousseau with the fact that he is himself a writer. This is so, says Rousseau; now I wish to save others from falling into the errors I fell into. 'I do not write to excuse my faults but to prevent readers from imitating them'* —a comment which anticipates The Confessions.

[2] *This comment obviously trades upon the previous implication that government is in the hands of rascals.*

bute to talent what is the effect of a moment and to take as a decided inclination towards this or that art the imitativeness that is common to men and monkeys, which impels both mechanically to wish to do what they see being done without knowing why it is good. The world is full of artisans and overfull of artists who possess no natural talent for the art they practise and into which they were pushed at an early age, either at the urging of others or because others saw in an apparent enthusiasm signs of true artistry which would, in fact, have led them in any other direction but this. One hears a drum and believes he is a general; another sees a building and imagines himself as an architect. Each is attracted to that which he sees when he believes it to be esteemed.

There is a great deal of difference between taking pleasure in an occupation and actually having a talent for it. It calls for more careful observation than is usually supposed to be sure what is the true genius and the true taste of a child, for he displays his desires more plainly than his possibilities and we judge by the first instead of looking for the second. I wish some person of wisdom and understanding would provide us with a treatise on the art of observing children. This skill is one that it is most important to advance; neither parents nor teachers have yet mastered its first essentials. (I) 230/231. (V) 161/162.

These last two sentences are almost an aside to the main discussion and are of considerable interest. It is difficult to know whether Rousseau is here recommending himself in a subtle way as that person of wisdom and understanding, or whether, taking the remark on its face value, we can say that, for all the acuity of observation shown in much of *Émile*, the main purpose of the book is other than to provide the world with this treatise that is so badly needed. In view of the place of the book in Rousseau's general plan of work, the latter interpretation would seem the more reasonable one to adopt. However we may read into the remark an implication that here is at least a good example of what is required, for all that it is not the chief purpose of the work to provide an authoritative and definitive treatise of this nature.

After this all but parenthetical remark Rousseau returns again to the discussion of a trade. It is now becoming disproportionately long. There are more shifts, backtrackings and qualifications, together with anecdotes and illustrations.

But perhaps we are giving too much importance to the choice of trade.

To which of the trades which are open to us to adopt will he give such time as is necessary to make him a satisfactory workman? That is the real question.

Give a man a trade suitable to his sex and to a young man one suitable to both his sex and his age ... (I) 231. (V) 162.

Certain trades are ruled out as excluded from these categories of suitability. Sedentary employments such as tailoring are excluded. The last has the added disadvantage of being a woman's work since in involves sewing.

That he engages himself in one of the trades he thinks fit is well and good; if he is truly a eunuch then he is reduced to the state of men who dishonour their sex by entering trades unsuitable to it. Their choice proclaims an error of nature; correct it how you can for you can do no harm.

We learn from this that nature can sometimes make a mistake. It is a surprise to us.

I would forbid my pupil to engage in an unhealthy trade but not one which was painful or even perilous. They will call upon his power and courage and are proper occupations only for men; women do not lay claim to them; how then are men not shamed who encroach upon women's? (I) 232/233. (V) 162.

I feel I have said too much for my agreeable contemporaries but I sometimes allow myself to be carried away by the importance of the argument. If there is a man who is ashamed to work in the open when making use of an adze and clothed in a leather apron then I think no more of him than that he is a slave to opinion, ready to blush at what is perfectly all right immediately someone laughs at honest people. However let us allow parents their prejudices where they do not impair the judgment of the child. It is unnecessary to practise all the honest trades in order to honour all trades that are honest; it is sufficient that we do not consider any of them to be beneath us. When we have a choice which need be determined by no one but ourselves why should one not consult with oneself as to the most agreeable to one's inclinations amongst those of equal merit? Work with metal is useful; it may even be the most useful of all. Nevertheless, unless there is some special point, I would not have your son a blacksmith, locksmith or iron worker; I do not like the idea of seeing him at his forge as if a Cyclops. (I) 234. (V) 163.

Masonry and shoemaking are now ruled out as insufficiently clean. Mechanical trades, i.e. ones with very limited skill or variation of activity, are excluded.

All things considered the trade I would most wish to suit the taste of my pupil is that of the carpenter. It is clean; it is useful; one can use it in the home. It provides the body with exertion; it demands skill and application and in the fashioning of useful articles elegance and taste are not excluded.

When Émile learns his trade I shall want to learn it with him because I am sure that he will learn nothing well that we do not learn together. Both of us then will be apprentices, and we shall not expect to be treated as gentlemen but as true apprentices who are not there for fun. Why should we not be in earnest?

Unfortunately it will not be possible to spend all our time at work. We are not apprentice workmen, we are apprentice men; and the apprenticeship to the latter trade is longer and more laborious than that of the former. What shall we do then? Take on a plane master for an hour a day much as one takes on a dancing master? No! We should become disciples not apprentices and our ambition is not so much to learn carpentry as to learn what it is to be a carpenter. I would have it that we go once or twice a week to spend the whole day at the place of the master, keeping his hours and getting to work before he does, that we eat at his table and work under his direction, and that, after having had the honour of sharing supper with his family we may return, if we wish, to our own hard beds. This is how one learns many trades at once; and how to work with one's hands without neglecting the other apprenticeship. (I) 234/235. (V) 164.

Emile will not receive wages for his work; this would ruin the purpose of the whole project. He would then be working for what was worthless in itself at the expense of valuing the work for its own sake.

Never judge his work except against the standards of a master. His work is to be appraised in terms of the work and not because it is work that *he* did. Say of that which is well done, 'Now that is good' but do not add, 'Who did it?' If he himself says proudly and contentedly; 'It was I who did that,' answer coolly, 'You or another, it is not important; it is still a good piece of work.' (I) 235. (V) 164.

If it was once thought a fashionable thing to do to have a trade, your children would soon have one without learning it; they would be designated masters like the councillors of Zurich. No such ceremony for Émile; nothing that is show and everything that is reality.

Don't proclaim his knowledge but let him learn in silence. Let him make his masterpiece but not to be titled master so that he does not reveal himself a workman by his title but by his work.

If I have contrived to make myself clear to this point, the reader should understand how, with the habit of exercising the body and using the hands, I have given my pupil, without his realising, a taste for reflection and meditation which counteracts in him the idleness which could result from his indifference to the judgments of others and his still unaroused passions. He works as a peasant and thinks as a philosopher, otherwise he is idle as a savage. The great secret of education is to ensure that the exercise of the body and the exercise of the mind should serve each other as relaxations.

But in our teaching let us guard against anticipating a mind more mature than it is. Émile will not long be at work before he experiences for himself the inequalities of condition he had not before perceived. He will want to examine me in my turn on those maxims he has accepted from me. Having received all these and finding himself so near to the state of the poor he will want to know why I am so far from it. He may put to me questions more scathing than he realises. 'You are rich you have told me and I have seen. A rich man owes his work to the society because he is a man. But you; what do you do for it?' What does the fine tutor say to this? I don't know. Perhaps he would be foolish to talk of the service he gives to the child. So far as I am concerned the workshop will help me out of the problem. 'That is an excellent question, my dear Émile; I promise to answer for myself when you can give a satisfactory answer for yourself. In the meantime I take care to render to you and to the poor all that I can manage, and to make a table or a bench each week in order not to be completely useless.'

We have returned to ourselves. The child is all but ready to cease to be a child now that he has hold of himself ... we have made of him a worker and a thinker; all that is left for us to achieve is to make of him a loving and sensitive man; which is to say perfect reason through feeling. But before we enter upon this new order of things, let us review what we have done and see as clearly as possible how far we have come.

Our pupil had only sensations at first, now he has some ideas; he could only feel, now he thinks. Because of the many sensations, both successive and simultaneous, and the judgment made upon them, there is born a kind of sensation, mixed or complex, which I call an idea.

The manner of formation of these ideas is that which gives a character to the human mind. The mind which forms ideas only from actual relations is a sound mind; the one content with apparent relations is a superficial mind; the one which sees relations as they are is a precise mind; the one which estimates badly is a false mind. To forge imaginary relations without foundation in reality is to be mad, to have none to compare is to be an imbecile. A greater or lesser aptitude to compare ideas and discover their relationships is that which makes a man greater or lesser of mind, etc. (I) 236/237. (V) 165.

Since all our errors stem from our judgments it is clear that if we had no need of judgment we should have no need to learn, we should never be in a state of delusion; we should be happier in our ignorance than we are able to be in our knowledge. Who can deny that a savant knows a thousand things which the ignorant do not? For all that are the savants any nearer the truth? Quite the contrary; the farther they advance the farther they move from the truth, because their vanity in their judgment outstrips their increase of insight; each truth they learn is accompanied by a hundred false judgments. Evidence of this last is that the learned societies of Europe are merely common schools of falsehood; and it is certain that there are more misapprehensions in the Academy of Sciences than in a whole tribe of Red Indians.

Since the more men know the more mistakes they make the only way to avoid error is to remain in ignorance. Make no judgments and you will never be deluded. This is the lesson of nature and, equally, of reason. Save for those immediate relations which are very few in number and which are of things of which we are most sensible, we have, for all the rest, a natural and profound indifference. A savage will not turn his head to see the working of the most beautiful machine nor for all the marvels of electricity. 'Of what importance to me?' is the most familiar saying of the ignorant and the most suitable one for the wise. But unfortunately this saying will serve us no more. Everything is of importance to us since we are dependent upon everything, and our curiosity must grow with our needs. This is why I attribute much of it to the philosopher and give none to the savage; the former has a need for everyone, admirers above all. You will say to me that I venture beyond nature; I do not believe so. She chooses her instruments and relies not upon opinion but upon need. Now a man's needs alter according to his situation. There is a tremendous difference between a natural man living in a state of nature and a natural man living in a society. Émile is not a savage to be relegated to the deserts; he is a savage who must live in towns. He must know how to provide for himself there, how to make use of the inhabitants, and to live with them even though not as they are.

Since we are in the midst of so many new relations and dependent upon them he must make judgments in spite of himself; teach him to judge well then.

The best way to learn to think with precision is that which tends to most simplify our sensations and even to discount them without falling into error. From this it follows that after becoming accustomed to checking one sense impression against that of another, one must now learn to verify the impressions of one sense by itself without needing to have recourse to another, whereupon each sensation yields an idea for us and this idea will always be a true one. This is the sort of gain I have attempted to gather in this third stage of human life. This manner of proceeding exacts a patience and circumspection which few teachers possess and without which the pupil will never learn to reason. (I) 239/240. (V) 167.

Rousseau now refers back to an example he had used earlier, that of the way which a stick looks as if bent or broken when partly immersed in water.

The stick, which is immersed to half its length in the water, is fixed in a perpendicular position. To know that it is broken as it appears to be have we not many things to do before we draw it from the water or touch it with a hand?

1. Firstly we move right around the stick and we see that the break turns with us. Then it is only our eye which makes the change for looks never moved anything.

2. We look directly down on the end of the stick that is above water; then the stick is no longer bent; the end nearest our eye precisely obscures the other end. Has our eye straightened the stick?[1]

3. We agitate the surface of the water; we see the stick break into many pieces; it moves in zig-zags and follows the undulations of the water. The movement we have given to the water is sufficient to break, soften and melt the stick?

4. We drain the water and we see the stick straighten, little by little as the level of the water descends. Isn't this more than enough to make the facts clear and to reveal the phenomena of refraction? It is just not true that the eye deceives us, since we have had no need to have recourse to anything else to rectify the errors attributed to it.[2]

Suppose the child were so stupid as to be unable to see this conclusion as the result of his experiences then you must appeal to touch to come to the aid of sight. Instead of removing the stick from the water, allow it to remain in its position and have the child pass his hand down it from one end to the other; he will feel no angularity; the stick is not broken then. You will say to me that it is not solely a matter of making judgments that is involved here but of formal reasoning. That is true, but do you not see that, as soon as the mind has acquired any ideas, all judgment is reasoning? The perception of any sensation consists in a proposition, a judgment. Accordingly, as soon as one compares one sensation with another, one reasons. The art of judging and the art of reasoning are exactly the same. (I) 241/242. (V) 168/169.

[1] *In a footnote Rousseau acknowledges the inaccuracy of this, but says it is of no great moment.*
[2] *This is remarkably like the conclusion arrived at by J. L. Austin in respect of the same problem. See* Sense and Sensibilia, *O.U.P., 1962.*

This passage has some problems. It contains much that is valid, particularly the implicit suggestion that a conceptual framework is essential before one can talk of mental operations that conform to established rules of some sort. We may, however, be somewhat bemused as to how there could be talk of judgment *before* this is supposed as possible to the child, as has been the case with Rousseau's account. One possibility is in the ambiguity of the term 'Judgment'.[1] Earlier it may have been used to indicate opinion or view—how something strikes the child as it were. Now it could be that it is used in a stricter sense. If this were so it would seem something of a pity that the identification of judgment with reason should have been quite so tersely made. Secondly, it would seem that this comment might well have been made much sooner in the third book, since examples are given at these earlier stages which plainly illustrate the general point now made.

> People argue over the choice of analysis or synthesis for studying science; it is not always necessary to choose at all. Sometimes one is able to solve a problem and to construct a theory in the same research, and to guide the child by instructing him when he believes he is only investigating or analysing. By using both methods at the same time each serves as a confirmation of the other's findings. Starting at opposite points without thinking of taking the same direction it will come as a surprise to arrive at a meeting point, and the surprise can only be an extremely agreeable one. I would wish, for example, to take Geography from two such angles, combining the study of the revolutions of the globe and the measurement of its proportions, starting with an initial study of the place in which one lives. Whilst the child studies the earth and its movements in space, bring him back to the divisions of the earth and show him his position on it.
>
> His two starting points in Geography will be the town where he lives and his father's country house; then the places between these two; next, the neighbouring rivers, and then the aspect of the sun and the path that it follows, that one may find one's way by it. Here is the meeting point. It is most desirable that he should make a map of all this; a very simple map, showing two things only at first, to which he gradually adds others as soon as he knows, or can guess, their relative positions. You will have seen already what a great advantage we have given him from the outset in showing him how to use his eyes as a compass. (I) 190. (V) 133.

The two examples are linked by an early and governing observation which both conform to.

[1] 'Vous me direz qu'il n'y a pas seulement ici des jugements, mais des raisonnements en forme.'

I have no love for explications in words; young people pay little heed to them and neither do they retain them very long. The thing! The thing! I cannot repeat it too often that we attribute too much to what words can do; with our educational babble we only fashion babblers. (I) 203. (V) 142.

Here we find the reasons why certain areas of study are not included in this phase of Émile's education; there are no 'things' which can be pointed to. Mention of these is included in the concluding passage to the third book, which, once more, takes the form of a sort of educational assessment of the pupil.

But you may take fright perhaps at the quantity of things that I have put before him. You fear I have crushed his mind under a multitude of ideas. It is quite to the contrary; rather I am teaching him to be ignorant of them than to know them. I am showing him the path of knowledge; an easy one it is true but one which is long, boundless and slow to travel. I am taking him the first exploratory steps but I am not allowing him to go far.

Forced to learn for himself, he uses his own reason and not that of others; to be independent of mere opinion it is necessary to be independent of authority. The greater part of our mistakes stem less from ourselves than from others. (I) 242. (V) 169.

Émile knows little but what he knows is truly his; he has no half knowledge. Of the small number of things that he knows and knows well the most important is that there is much of which he is ignorant and can come to know one day, much more that other men know which he will never know, and an infinite amount that no man will ever know. He has a wide ranging mind, not because of its store of information but because of his ability to acquire it; an open mind; intelligent; ready for anything, and as Montaigne said, if not instructed at least instructable. I am content that he should know the 'Wherefore' of all he does and the 'Why' of all he believes.

Émile's knowledge is of nature and the purely material alone. He does not even know the name of History nor that of Metaphysics or Morals. He knows the essential relationships between men and things but nothing of the moral relationships between man and man. He knows little of generalising and of how to make abstractions. He sees that certain qualities are common to certain things without reasoning over these qualities themselves. . . . He does not search into the nature of things but only into the relationships that affect him.

Émile is hardworking, even tempered, patient, persistent, full of courage. His imagination, quite uninflamed, enlarges nothing into a danger; he feels few ills and these he suffers with equanimity because he has not learnt to dispute fate. (I) 243. (V) 169.

In a word Émile has efficacy in all that concerns himself. To possess a social efficacy also he lacks only the knowledge of the relations which demand it; he lacks only the insights which his mind is ready to receive.

He considers himself without regard to others and finds it good that others should think little about him. He exacts nothing from anyone and believes he owes nothing to anyone. He is alone in the midst of human society and counts on no one but himself; for he is all that one is able to be at his age. He has no errors or only those inevitable to all of us; he has no vices or only those from which no man can protect himself. He has a healthy body with agile limbs, a precise mind free of prejudice; his heart is free and without passions. Respect of self, the first and most natural of all, is as yet scarcely active. Without troubling the peace of others he has lived content, happy and free to the extent that nature permits. Do you consider that a child attaining fifteen years of age thus, has lost anything of his time? (I) 244. (V) 170.

Chapter Four

OF MAN TO MAN

The opening to the fourth book of *Émile* is melodramatic.

With what swiftness life passes here below!

It sets the tone for the whole of this very large section of the total work in that it is a statement of great generality. From this point on the nature of the work changes. There is progressively less reference to Émile or to what would now be called 'practical examples', such as the investigation of the stick placed in water. There is an increase in the use of terms such as 'a child', 'the child' and 'man'. The term 'society' makes its appearance in a somewhat different context than hitherto. Previously it was used mainly to refer to the source of error and the area where change was most required. From this point it comes under examination in terms of its development, its fundamental characteristics and its significance for man.

It was pointed out in the Introduction that Rousseau had once intended to produce a comprehensive single work which would have embodied the whole of his thinking. It is probable that, out of this, emerged both *Émile ou de l'education* and *The Social Contract*. It was also explained that the two books were published separately by different publishers rather than as was intended, namely as complements the one to the other. Now *Social Contract* is a small work, generally terse in expression and sometimes severely economical in argument. It contains a number of central concepts of considerable complexity, among these being *'amour de soi'* and *'amour propre'* and those of 'the will of all' and 'the general will'; all of them being objects of very considerable philosophical discussion and puzzlement.[1]

[1] *See* Rousseau; A Study of his Thought, *J. H. Broome, Arnold, 1963, for an excellent discussion of all this.*

But it is not in 'Social Contract' alone that these concepts are embodied and not in that work alone that they are supposedly argued and explicated. Much of the fourth book of Émile could be transported into the Social Contract as supporting argument and clarification to that work's general thesis. It is plain that Rousseau, by the time he had reached this point in Émile, was concerned far more with a general social and political position than with the education of children. The usefulness of the device of an imaginary pupil and a hypothetical tutor is all but exhausted.

This is not to say that the book does not still contain some important insights of a psychological nature, particularly with reference to the adolescent. The chief concerns in this respect are those of the arousal of the passions and of the relationships between men which Rousseau has, until now sought to preserve from the child's acquaintance as a study. All this is ancillary to the main purpose of the book, however. Preserved as if in a state of nature until upon the very threshold of manhood, Émile is now treated as fitted to construct a new and better society by virtue of the fact that his preservation has kept from him the corruptions of the old. He can understand and further a sound ethical plan for living in association with his fellows.

One section of the fourth book consists in a delineation of what is to be meant by the often employed expression, 'the author of nature'. It is separately titled The Creed of a Savoyard Priest and is really an exposition of Rousseau's position in respect of a Deity. This had to come somewhere in the general plan of Rousseau's work for the reasons that are set out in the Introduction. It appears in Émile because it fits in with some convenience in respect of the obvious question as to what a young man is to be taught about the existence or non-existence of a God and what sort of God exists if He does exist.

The fourth book is almost as long as the three preceding books put together. In a work of this compass it would be neither possible nor appropriate to treat of it in relation to its size. What the difference indicates is the relation between Rousseau's work on Education and his overall purpose. It is almost possible to say that he has completed one task and commenced a second and larger one at the beginning of this part of Émile.

The problem is stated in the rest of the first paragraph.

The first quarter of life is gone before we know how to use it; the last quarter is lived after we are able to enjoy it. At first we know nothing of living; soon we are no longer able to use our knowledge; and in the interval which separates these two extremes of uselessness three quarters of the time is consumed by sleep, by work, by sorrows, restrictions and every sort of pain. Life is short, less because of the little duration it has but because so little of this time is ours to enjoy. From birth to death is a long enough time: life is always too short when the time between is empty of reward.

The solution is a many sided one:

We are born twice as it were; the first time into existence; the second time into life; the first time for the species; the second as man or woman. Those who regard woman as an imperfect man are undoubtedly unjust and prejudiced, but external appearance is on their side. Until the age of sexual maturity children of both sexes are indistinguishable; same facial appearance; same figure, same colouring, voice; everything is similar in appearance; both boys and girls are children; the same description suffices for both. Males whose development is arrested in respect of their sex retain this same conformity of appearance all their lives; they are always big children just as women who do not lose this sameness resemble, in many respects, nothing else but that. But man in general is not made to remain a perpetual child. He leaves it at a time prescribed by nature, and this moment of crisis, short in itself, has far reaching influence. (I) 245. (V) 172.

In the paragraph that follows Rousseau characterises the 'moment of crisis as one of tempestuousness of mind and emotion, rebellion and refusal to follow where once he would obey.

To the moral indications of a change in temperament are added perceptible changes of figure. His physique develops and takes the imprint of his character; the scanty down about his chin and cheeks becomes darker and thicker. His voice breaks or he loses it completely; he is neither child nor man and cannot take the tone of voice of either. His eyes, those organs of the spirit, which have said nothing until this time, find a language and an expression; a newborn fire illuminates them, their ever more ardent gaze retains a sacred innocence but they no longer have their prior vacancy; he is uneasily aware that they can say too much; he begins to know what it is to hide them and blush; he has feelings which he cannot identify and is uneasy without knowing why. All this may come slowly and allow you time, but if his sense of life makes him impatient; if his fits of passion reach madness, if he is angry and contrite all but at the same time, if he bursts into tears without reason, if the proximity of objects which could be dangerous quickens his pulse and brightens his eye, if a woman's hand upon his own sets him trembling, if he is troubled or diffident in her presence, Ulysses, oh wise Ulysses have a care for yourself! (I) 245. (V) 172.

This is the time of the second birth of which I spoke; it is now that a man truly enters into life and that nothing that is of a human being remains a stranger to him. Till now our cares have been as child's play; now they are of real importance. This stage of living, when it is customary for education to end, is properly the one when we ought to begin; but in order to make this new plan clear let us return to the state of things where we left it.

Our passions are the principal instruments of our preservation; it is therefore both impossible and ridiculous to wish to destroy them for it would be to command nature and to improve upon the work of God Himself. . . . I find those who wish to obstruct the emergence of the passions to be about as foolish as those who would destroy them and those who believe that such has been my object up to this point have badly misunderstood me.

But is it sound argument to contend that, if it is in the nature of man to have passions, we can conclude that all the passions which we experience in ourselves and observe in others are natural? Their origin is natural it is true but a thousand foreign streams have swollen them; they are a great flood, constantly growing, and in which one can discover hardly a drop of the original. Our natural passions are very limited; they are instruments of our freedom; they tend to preserve us. All those which subjugate us and destroy us come to us from elsewhere. Nature does not give them to us; we appropriate them to the detriment of nature.

The source of our passions, the origin and the principle of all the others, the only one which is born with man and which never leaves him whilst he lives, is love of self:[1] a primitive passion, innate, preceding all others; indeed in one sense, all the others are merely modifications derived from non-natural influences, without whose presence the changes would not have occurred; and these same modifications, far from being to our advantage, are detrimental; they alter the prime purpose of the passions and work contra to their principle; in this way man finds himself out of nature and at odds with himself.

Love of self is always good and always in conformity with nature. Each individual is especially charged to care for his own preservation, of which responsibility the most important care is and must be constant vigilance for life itself, and how can this be achieved if we do not take the greatest interest in it?

It follows from this that to preserve ourselves is to love ourselves and to love ourselves above everything. From this it follows immediately that we love that which is preservative of ourselves. All infants become attached to their nurses; Romulus must have become attached to the wolf who suckled him. At first this bond is purely instinctive. That which favours the well being of an individual draws him,[2] that which is harmful repels; it is nothing but blind instinct. That which

---

[1] 'l'amour de soi'.

[2] *Lorenz in* King Solomon's Ring *confirms this instinctive attraction.*

transforms this instinct into a sentiment, the attachment into love, the aversion into hatred, is an evident intention of harming or benefitting us. One does not become impassioned with insensible objects which only follow the impetus they are given, but those of which one expects benefit or harm as a consequence of their internal disposition, of their volition, those which we consider to act independently for or against us inspire in us sentiments similar to those they show to us. Something is to our benefit, we seek it; but he who wishes to serve us we love. That which harms us we shrink from; he who wishes us harm, we hate. (I) 248. (V) 173.

The first sentiment of a child is love of himself; the second, which has its derivation in the first, is love of those who most nearly affect him, because in the state of helplessness of an infant he knows of other people only the care and the assistance received from them. At first his attachment for his nurse and governess is a mere habit. He seeks them because he has need of them and because he feels good with them near him; it is more a matter of perception than of sentiment. It takes him a long time to realise that not only are they useful to him but that they wish to be; it is then that he begins to love them.

A child then is naturally inclined to goodwill, because he finds that all who are near to him tend to assist him. He forms from this perception a habit of favourable regard for all people; but in ratio with the extension of his relationships, his needs, his dependence, active or passive, his appraisal of his relationships with others is awakened and produces notions of obligation and preference. Then the child becomes imperious, jealous, deceitful and vindictive. If his obedience is required and he does not see the usefulness of that which he is commanded to do, he attributes it to caprice, to an intention to torment him, and he rebels. If people obey him, then, when something resists him, he sees that as rebellion, an intention to resist him; he beats the chair or the table for disobedience. Love of self (*amour de soi*) applies only to ourselves and is content when our real needs are satisfied ; but selfishness (*amour propre*) which is comparative, is never content and could not be because this sentiment which prefers self to others, requires also that others prefer this self to themselves and this is impossible. Now it can be seen that the sweet and tender passions arise from love of self and the hateful and violent arise from selfishness. Thus that which makes man essentially good is the small number of needs he has and the little need to compare himself with others; that which makes man essentially evil are many needs and much reliance upon the opinion of others. On this principle it is easy to see how one is able to control to the good or to the bad all the passions of children and of men. It is true that, being unable always to live alone they find it difficult always to be good. This difficulty is necessarily increased as their relationships increase. It is this fact which, above all, makes it essential that the dangers of society be guarded against with art and skill so that depravity, spawned by fresh needs, be not born in the human heart.

Man's proper study is that of his relationship with the world. So long as he only knows of it through his physical contacts, he should study himself in relation to things and this is the occupation for childhood; when he begins to become aware of his moral being he should study himself in relation to other men; this is an occupation for a lifetime, beginning at the stage we have now reached. (I) 248/249. (V) 174/175.

There is one point of interest about this passage which might not be immediately apparent. Rousseau has arrived at the conclusion that man is by nature of a good will in his attitude to others. He has done this by psychological observation. Later on Immanuel Kant was to advance a celebrated argument which has at its base the premiss that the only thing that is good without any qualification is a good will.[1] What is of interest is that Kant was much interested in Rousseau's political and educational writings and must have been very familiar with the psychological and experimental argument advanced by him in the passage immediately above.

However different the purposes and the cast of thought possessed by the two men, this historical link exists.

'At the stage we have now reached', Rousseau quickly looks to the future and to the dawning of love between man and woman, which, he contends, is a product of reason and comparison, hence the care and the difficulty inbuilt in loving.

Far from it being the case that love comes from nature, it is the regulator and curb of her inclinations; it is through love that, the loved one excepted, one sex is as nothing to the other.

The preference we accord we wish to be accorded to us; love must be reciprocal. To be loved one must make oneself loveable; to be preferred one must make oneself more loveable than any other, at least in the eyes of the one beloved. For this reason the first regard is for our fellows and the first comparisons are with them; for this reason there arises emulation, rivalry and jealousy. A heart full to overflowing with feeling, yearns to unburden itself; from want of mistress is born want of a friend. He who knows how sweet it is to be loved, desires to be loved by all, and there could be no preferences were it not that many go unsatisfied. With love and friendship come dissensions, enmity and hate. At the heart of all these diverse passions I see, implacably enthroned, the power of opinion, and foolish men enslaved by her, rest their very existence on the judgment of others.

Extend these ideas and you will see from whence comes the selfishness which is believed to be natural and how love of self ceases to

[1] See 'Groundwork of the Metaphysic of Morals', *translated Paton, Harper Torchbooks 1964.*

be an independent sentiment, becoming pride in great minds, vanity in little ones; all of which feeds itself constantly at the cost of one's fellows. This sort of passion, having no germ in the heart of the infant, does not rise there of itself; it is we who plant them there and they would never take root but by our fault. This is not so of the young man however; whatever we do they will arise in him. It is therefore time to change our methods. (I) 250. (V) 175/176.

The teaching of nature is slow and long; that of man is almost invariably premature. In the former the senses awaken the imagination; in the latter the imagination awakens the senses. . . . Children have singular sagacity in teasing out the tricks of decency which cloak immorality. The refined language one uses, the lessons in decency one gives them, the veil of mystery you take on before them are nothing but incitements to their curiosity. From the manner you assume it is clear that what you hide from them is that which they are to learn, and, of all the teaching you give them, they profit the most from this.

Consult experience; you will understand the extent to which this senseless method accelerates the work of nature and ruins the character. This is one of the principal causes of degeneration among townspeople. The young folk, drained of their strength, stay small, feeble, misinformed, aged instead of growing; as a vine made to bear fruit in springtime languishes and dies before the autumn.

One has to live among rough and simple people to understand how long a happy ignorance can prolong the innocence of children. (I) 252. (V) 177.

Neither retard nor accelerate sexual awareness is Rousseau's plea. To accelerate it is to vitiate the species; to retard it is merely to bottle it up unhealthily.

From these reflections I came to the answer to that question so frequently aired; is it a good thing to explain that which excites the curiosity of children at an early age or is it better to quiet it with the lies of modesty? I think there is no need to do either the one or the other. Firstly, this curiosity does not arise in them unless it has been stimulated. Care should be taken that this does not happen. Secondly, questions which one is not forced to answer do not require us to deceive those who ask them; it is better to impose silence upon a child than it is to answer him with an untruth. . . . Finally, should you decide to answer him, do so with the greatest simplicity, without mystery, embarrassment and with all seriousness. There is much less danger in satisfying the curiosity of a child than there is in exciting it.

Your answers should be grave, short, definite and without hint of hesitation. I have no need to add that they ought always to be true. It is not possible to teach children the danger of lying to people unless for their part, people realise the danger of lying to children. A single untruth from the master to the pupil ruins for ever all the fruits of education.

I do not like those who affect too sophisticated a manner of speech with children, nor should they be tediously devious in their, (inevitably detected), attempts to avoid calling things by their true names. Good manners in these matters are always as simple as possible; but an imagination sullied by vice makes for an oversensitive ear and compels us to constant refinement of expression. Plain words do no harm; it is lasciviousness which must be cast out.

Although modesty is natural to the human being, children are not naturally possessed of it. Modesty only comes with the knowledge of evil; how should children who neither have nor should be allowed to have this understanding, possess the sentiment which is its effect? To give them lessons in modesty and honesty is to teach them that there is shamefulness and dishonesty and to give them a secret desire to know of these things. Sooner or later they will come to the point, and the first spark which touches the imagination will certainly inflame the senses. Whoever blushes is already guilty; true innocence is ashamed of nothing. (I) 253/254. (V) 178.

I can see but one good means of preserving the innocence of children; it is that all those who surround him respect and love him. Without this all the discretion one might exercise is bound to fail sooner or later; a smile, a wink, a casual gesture will tell of everything which we have sought to hide from him; it is sufficient to teach him that there is something you wished to conceal from him. The delicacy of phrase and expression employed by mannered persons hints at insights which children should not have, which are out of place for them; but when we truly honour their lack of guile it becomes easy enough to talk with them in suitable terms. (I) 254. (V) 178.

If you wish to establish order and regulation among the rising passions, extend the time during which they develop in order that they have time to arrange themselves as they arise. In that case it is not man who orders them but nature herself; your care is to see that she is allowed to do her work. If your pupil were alone you would have nothing to do, but everything about him inflames his imagination. A tide of prejudice and opinion engulfs him; to hold it back one must push in the opposite direction. Feeling must restrain imagination; reason reduce to silence the prejudgments of men. The source of all the passions is sensibility; imagination determines their bent. Every being who is aware of his relations must be affected when these relationships change and when he perceives, or believes he does, others better suited to him. Errors of the imagination transform into vices the passions of all mortal men and even of angels, if they have passions. . . . (I) 256. (V) 180.

But has man the mastery that he can order his affections in conformity with this or that relation? Undoubtedly, if he is able to direct his imagination upon this or that object or to adopt this or that habit. Furthermore it concerns us less here whether a man is able to do this on his own than whether we are able to do something for our pupil by our choice of the circumstances. To show the proper means to maintain him in the order of nature is to show, too, how he might stray from it. (I) 257. (V) 181.

The first sentiment to which a well taught young man is susceptible is not that of love; it is friendship. The first act of his aroused imagination is to inform him of his fellows; the species affects him before sex does. Here is yet another advantage of prolonged innocence; profiting by his dawning sensibility one may sow the first seeds of humanity in his heart; the advantage is the more precious since this is the single time of life when the same efforts may be expected to meet with true success.

I have always noticed that young men, corrupted in early youth and given over to women and debauchery, become inhuman and cruel; their impetuous temperaments make them impatient, vindictive and violent; their imaginations, chained to a single object, refuse all others; they know nothing of pity or of mercy; they would sacrifice father, mother, the entire world to the least of their pleasures. Conversely, a young man brought up in happy simplicity is carried by the first movements of nature towards tenderness and affection; his compassionate heart is troubled by the sufferings of his fellows; he trembles with pleasure upon meeting his comrade; his arms know how to embrace with tenderness; his eyes can shed tears of compassion; he is sensitive to the shame of others' displeasure and regrets giving offence.... Adolescence is not the age of vengefulness or hatred; it is the age of sympathy, clemency and generosity. Yes; this is my contention and I have no fear that I will be falsified by experience. A child who is not base born and who retains his innocence until his twentieth year, is, at that age the most generous, the best, the most loving and the most lovable of human beings. You have never heard anything of the sort? I can well believe it; you philosophers, brought up and educated in all the corruption of our colleges, have no knowledge of this.

It is the weakness of man which makes him sociable; our common misery draws our hearts to humanity in general; we should owe nothing to it were we not men ourselves. All attachment is a sign of insufficiency; if each of us had no need of others we should scarcely think of making ourselves at one with them. Thus it is that out of our infirmity is born our precarious happiness. A truly happy man is a solitary man; God alone enjoys absolute happiness; which of us has any idea of what that state might be? (I) 258/259. (V) 182.

It follows that we form attachments to our fellows less from consideration of their pleasure than of that which causes them sorrow, because we then recognise most clearly a being like ourselves and a

E

warranty for their attachment to us. If our common needs unite us
in our interests, our common misery unites us in affection. The sight
of a happy man inspires in others less of love than of envy; we are
prone to accuse him of usurping a right which is not his in keeping
happiness for himself, and selfishness is further outraged when we
realise that this man has no need of us.

To excite and nourish in the heart of a young man the first stirrings
of an awakening sensitivity and to form his character in the ways of
charitableness and goodness, avoid planting the seeds of pride, vanity,
and envy in him by presenting him with a bogus picture of human
happiness; do not parade the pomp of courts before his eyes, the
splendour of palaces, the attractions of pageantry, nor allow him to
move in fashionable circles and attend brilliant assemblies; do not
show him the exterior aspects of society until after he is capable of
assessing it as itself. To show him the world before he understands
men is not to instruct but to mislead.

Men by nature are not kings, princes, courtiers, nor are they rich;
all are naked and poor; all subject to the miseries of life, to its regrets
and inconveniences, its maladies, needs and sorrows of all kinds, and,
finally, all are condemned to die. This is the true condition of man and
no man is exempt from it. Begin the study of human nature by looking at that which is inseparable from it, that which is most accurately
defining of humanity. At sixteen the adolescent knows what it is to
suffer because he has suffered himself; but he scarcely realises that
others suffer also. To see without feeling is not to know, and, as I
have said a hundred times, the child cannot imagine the feelings of
others and so can know no ills but his own; but when the developing
sensibility illumines the imagination he begins to perceive himself in
his fellows, to be moved by their cries and to suffer their sadness. It
is at this time that the sad spectacle of suffering humanity should
bring to his heart the first pangs of compassion he has ever experienced.

If this occurrence is not easily observed in your children who is to
blame? You were so quick to teach them to play at feeling; you taught
them the language of feeling so early that, talking always in that same
tone, they turn your lessons against yourself and allow you no
opportunity to distinguish when they stop pretending and begin to
feel what they say. But look at my Émile. Up to this time I have led
him neither to feel nor to pretend to feel. Before knowing what it is
to feel the emotion of love he has never said, 'I love you very much' to
anyone; no one has taught him what expression he ought to assume
upon entering the room of his mother or father or sick tutor; no one
has shown him the art of affecting a sorrow he does not feel.…
Indifferent to all but himself, as are all other infants, he takes no
interest in others: all that distinguishes him from the rest is that he
makes no pretence at interest and that he is not false as they are.

Having thus thought little about sensible beings it will be late before Émile comes to an understanding of suffering and death. Complaints and cries will then begin to stir his heart; the sight of blood will cause him to avert his eyes; the paroxysms of a dying animal will arouse in him I know not what anguish before he understands what explains these strange movements. If he remained stupid and barbaric he would not experience such feeling; had he been more informed he would have known their cause; he has previously compared ideas frequently enough not to be without feeling but insufficiently to know what he feels.

Thus pity is born, the first sentiment relative to others to touch the human heart according to the order of nature. (I) 260/261/262. (V) 183/184.

The sympathetic imagination is now fully awakened and undistorted by any premature elicitation of it. What must now be done is to allow of its exercise? Rousseau, at this point, issues three further guiding maxims.

FIRST MAXIM

It is not in the human heart to take the place of people who are happier than ourselves but only of those who are deserving of pity.

If one finds exceptions to this maxim they are more apparent than real.... Sometimes the rich man is loved when plunged into misfortune, but whilst he prospers he has no true friend but the one undeceived by appearances and who pities rather than envies him despite his prosperity. (I) 262. (V) 184.

SECOND MAXIM

We pity no misfortune of another's from which we believe ourselves to be exempt.

I know nothing so fine, profound, touching, and so true as this is. Why are kings without pity for their subjects? It is because they do not count themselves as ordinary men. Why are rich people so harsh to the poor? It is because they have no fear of becoming poor themselves. Why have the aristocracy such contempt for the people? Because a nobleman cannot be lowly born.

Do not let your pupil form the habit of looking down from the height of his pride upon the sufferings of the unfortunate, the labourings of the miserable, and do not hope to teach him to consider them in others if he considers them as foreign to himself. Make him well aware that the condition of these unfortunates can be his own; that a thousand happenings may plunge him in a moment, unexpectedly and inevitably, into all their unhappiness. Teach him to take no account of birth, health or fortune; show him all the vicissitudes of chance. (I) 263. (V) 185.

THIRD MAXIM

The pity we feel for others is in ratio not with the magnitude of the misfortune but with the feelings we attribute to the sufferer.

One only pities the unfortunate to the extent that one believes they find themselves in need of pity. The physical effects of our misfortunes are more limited than they seem; it is memory which continues them and imagination which extends them into the future and makes us truly pitiable.... In general I judge the extent to which any man prizes the happiness of his fellows by what he appears to think of them.

In a word teach your pupil to love everybody, even those who disparage him, to behave in no way as if a member of one particular class but find a place amongst all. Talk with tenderness of human beings when with him, with pity even, but never with disdain. As a man never dishonour mankind. (I) 264/265. (V) 186.

By now the concepts of self love and selfishness have been carefully distinguished. The tenor of Rousseau's argument has been to allow the first to develop as, it is contended, it surely will, while taking every step to prevent the growth of the latter. That he does not now go on to detail any procedures for securing this end has already been remarked upon with respect to the level of generality of this book of *Émile*. Very shortly after the passages quoted above Rousseau himself makes the comment:

This is the spirit of the method that is precribed. Here examples and details are of no value because at this stage begins the almost infinite division of character among people so that each example I gave would, perhaps, be suitable for one person in a hundred thousand. (I) 266. (V) 187.

In the Introduction it was pointed out that Rousseau did not recommend an education which shielded the pupil from adversities or unpleasantness. At this point in his work it is plain that it is a central feature of the young man's education that he should become acquainted with misfortune. Rousseau feels it necessary to comment on this:

... Without doubt more than one reader will reproach me for my forgetfulness of my first resolutions and the lasting happiness I have promised to my pupil. The wretched, the dying, scenes of sorrow and misery, what happiness or joy here for a young heart at the beginning of life! His mournful tutor, who has purposed so gentle an education, only brings him that which arouses suffering. This is what people will say but why should I care? I have promised to make him happy not to appear happy. Is it my fault if, deceived as always by appearances, you take them to be the reality. (I) 268. (V) 188.

Rousseau now turns to the problems of dealing with the young of this age:

> Teachers complain that the turbulence of this age makes the young ungovernable, and I observe this; but is it not the case that the teachers are at fault? As soon as this energy has been allowed to flow through the senses do they not understand that it is not possible to divert it? Will long, cold, sermonisings by pedants efface from the mind of the pupil the memory of pleasures he has conceived, banish from his heart desires which torment him, kill the ardour of a temperament that he knows how to use? Will he not batter himself against the obstacles which oppose him in the only happiness of which he has an idea? In the harsh law imposed upon him without his understanding how could he not see the caprice and hatred of people who seek ways to torment him? Is it strange that he rebels and hates everyone about him?
>
> I am well aware that, by being rather easy, one makes oneself tolerated and can keep an apparent authority, but I cannot see at all the value of an authority which is only maintained over a pupil by fomenting the vices it should prevent; this is to calm a fiery horse by making it leap over a precipice!
>
> Far from the energy of an adolescent being an obstacle to his education, this passionate involvement is that which brings it to consummation and achievement; it is that which can win for you the prize of a young man's heart when he ceases to be less strong than you are. His first affections are the reins by which you direct all his movements; he was free but I see him reduced to servitude. So long as he loved nothing he was dependent upon himself alone and his own needs; as soon as he loves he is dependent upon his attachments. Thus he forms the first ties which unite him with his species. However, in directing his growing sensibility in this way do not believe that it will be to embrace all men or that the word 'humanity' will have any significance for him. No; this sensibility will at first be limited to those like himself, or those not unknown to him; they are his familiars whom habit has made dear or necessary to him; those who plainly think and feel as he does; those he sees to have suffered the same pains and enjoyed the same pleasures as he; in a word those whose obvious similarities with him dispose him the more to love himself. It is not until after his natural self has been cultivated in a thousand ways, after much thought about his own feelings and those he observes in others, that he can succeed in generalising his individual notions under the abstract idea of humanity and unite with his own individual affections those which may unite him with his species. (I) 275/276. (V) 194.

My Émile, having until this time thought only of himself, when his regard first turns upon his fellows, he compares himself with them and the first feeling which is excited in him by this comparison is the desire to take first place. This is the point where love of self undergoes the change into selfishness and where arise all the passions stemmed from the latter. But in order to decide whether the passions which will predominate in his character will be those which are human and gentle or those which are cruel and malevolent, those of bene- volence and compassion or those of envy and covetousness, it is necessary to know how he feels he stands in relation to other men, and what kind of obstacles he believes he must surmount if he is to make his way to the position he wishes to occupy.

There is, in the state of nature, an equality that is real and indes- tructible, because it is impossible in that state that any difference between man and man could be great enough to make one dependent upon the other. There is, in the civil state, an equality of right which is chimerical and vain, because the means destined to maintain it, serve, of themselves, to destroy it, and the power of the community added to that of the strongest to oppress the weak disrupts the equili- brium that nature has established between men. (I) 279/280. (V) 197.

Rousseau has now introduced the basis for the second vital con- ceptual distinction upon which *The Social Contract* is founded, namely that between the 'general will' and the 'will of all'. To attempt to clarify this distinction is to undertake a task far too great for this book. Rousseau himself never succeeds in achieving a hard-and-fast division. It can be said, however, that the above quoted passage makes clear that which Rousseau finds objectionable and an impediment to human development; the elevation of organ- ised society over the sanctity of the individual man. In a footnote to the above he says:

The universal spirit of the laws of all countries always favours the strong over the weak, and he who has over he who has not: this disadvantage is inevitable and without exception. (I) 280. (V) 197.

The categorical assertion is not backed by argument in *Émile*. In the *Social Contract* Rousseau will seek to show, by somewhat curious historical analyses, that there is foundation for the claim.

From this first discrepancy flows all that which one can remark upon in the civil order where appearance and reality conflict. Always the many are sacrificed for the few and the common good to the particular interest; always there is specious employment of the names of justice and subordination as instruments of coercion and weapons of evil; thus it follows that the privileged claim usefulness to others when they are only advancing themselves at the cost of others; upon this we may claim the right to judge of their due according to justice and reason. It remains to be seen if the rank they have acquired for themselves is more favourable to happiness than the position in society we occupy, then each one of us can come to a judgment that is accurate as to his own lot. This is what concerns us; but, to do it well, we must start with an understanding of the human heart.

I would wish the company of a young man to be so chosen that he thinks well of those amongst whom he lives; and that you teach him to understand the world so well that he thinks badly of all that happens in it. He should know that man is naturally good; he should feel this; he should judge his neighbour by himself, but he should see how society depraves and perverts men and find in their prejudices the source of all their vices; he should come to value each individual but to despise the mass, that all men present nearly the same mask but that some faces are finer than the mask which covers them. (I) 281. (V) 198.

Capitalising upon all that has gone before, Rousseau is now well launched upon a social and political thesis and is lending it all the polemical power of which he is capable. For at least this moment Émile is left in the background. Rousseau is anticipating the work to be accomplished by *The Social Contract.* He continues to do this in what follows. In *The Social Contract,* as has already been remarked, a historical analysis is intended to substantiate the argument. To this point in *Émile* what remark upon the subject of history there has been has been proscriptive. It is now time for a change. (I) 282. (V) 199.

To understand men it is necessary to see what they do. In the world we hear what they say; they display their words and conceal their actions. In history they are unveiled and we can judge them by their deeds. Their sayings may assist us in appreciating them, because comparison of what they do and what they say shows us, at one and the same time, what they are and what they wish to appear to be; the more they disguise themselves the more one sees them as they are.

Unfortunately this study has dangers and detriments of more than one sort. It is difficult to take up a viewpoint from which one can judge fairly of one's fellows. One of the great faults of history is that it paints men more from their bad sides than from the good. Only revolutions and catastrophe hold the interest. When a people increases and prospers in the calm of peaceful governance history has nothing to say; she only remarks upon peoples who, no longer able to be self sufficient, intrude upon the affairs of neighbouring nations or permit that intrusion upon themselves; she depicts them only when they are in decline. All our histories begin where they should end. We have precise accounts of nations in ruin; that which we need is of nations in increase; they are so happy and so wise that history has nothing to say of them, and, in fact, we see, even now, that the governments which are most effective are those least talked of. We therefore know only of the bad; little of the good is mentioned of an epoch. The wicked become celebrated; the good are ignored or ridiculed. History, just as philosophy constantly blackens humanity.

You will say to me that accuracy in history is of less interest than true accounts of morals and character; if the human heart is faithfully represented it is of little moment that events are accurately reported. After all, you may add, what does it matter to us if something happened two thousand years ago? Reason is on your side if the portraits are really taken from nature, but if, for the most part, the model is to be in the imagination of the historian is this not to fall into the very error one wished to avoid, to give to the authority of the writer that which one withheld from the teacher? If my pupil is to see nothing but pictures drawn from fantasy I would much rather they were traced by my hand than by another's; they will, at least, be more appropriate to him.

The worst historians for a young man are those who make judgments. The facts! The facts![1] Let him judge for himself; it is thus that he will learn to understand mankind. If the judgment of the author constantly directs he will only be able to see through the eye of another, and when that eye fails him, he will see nothing.

History in general is defective in that it only remarks facts which are material and noteworthy and which can be fixed by names, places and dates; but the slow and ongoing reasons for the emergence of these facts, which are not amenable to chronicling in this way, always remain unknown. One frequently finds a battle lost or won to be the cause of a revolution, yet, even before this battle occurred, the revolution was inevitable. Historians rarely seem to see that war hardly does more than make manifest events which were priorly determined by moral causes. (I) 283/284/285. (V) 200/201.

Add to all these reflections that history is better at showing us actions than men because she seizes them in certain moments when they are clothed for exhibition; reveals only the public figure when he has arranged to be seen but does not follow him into his home, his study, amongst his family and with his friends; does no more than put him on show; paints his clothes more than his person.

I would far rather that a reading of particular lives should begin the study of the human heart,[2] for then the subject stands naked; the historian follows him everywhere, allowing him no moments out of sight, no corner where he can evade the spectator's piercing eye; it is when he believes he has hidden himself securely that the author can best distinguish him. (I) 285. (V) 201.

[1] *Rousseau appears to have forgotten that, earlier in the book, he had raised that most troublesome of questions, 'What is a fact?' It would be even more troublesome for him at this juncture!*

[2] *It will be remembered that Rousseau himself did precisely this at his father's knee.*

Few people seem able to realise the effect such reading, thus directed, is able to have upon the inexperienced mind of a young man. Dulled by the books of our infancy, accustomed to reading without thinking,[1] that which we read strikes us with ever lessening force, for carrying within us the passions and prejudices which crowd history and the lives of men, all that they do appears to us to be natural since we are far from the natural and judge others by ourselves. But picture to yourselves a young man taught in accordance with my maxims; think of my Émile, who, for eighteen years has been assiduously cared for with the sole object of preserving in him integrity of judgment and a healthy heart; imagine him, as the veil lifts, casting eyes for the first time upon the stage of the world, or rather upon the back of the stage, watching the actors take and don their costumes, counting the cords and pulleys by which great show abuses the eye of the spectator: soon his first surprise will be replaced by shame and disdain of his fellow man; he will be outraged to see how the whole species deceives itself with childish make believe; he will grieve over the sight of his brothers tearing at each other over dreams and changing themselves into wild animals because they were not content to be men.

Certainly with the natural dispositions of the pupil, if the master takes the least bit of care in his choice of reading, if he does anything at all to start him thinking about what he reads, the exercise will be, for him, a course of practical philosophy, entirely preferable and better understood than all the vain speculations with which one bruises the minds of young people in our schools. (I) 288. (V) 203/ 204.

Rousseau then recommends various readings which, fairly clearly, stem from his own childhood experience, and are expected to illustrate the contention that ambition is corruptive.

I have taken ambition for my example but the play of all human passions offers similar lessons to anyone who wishes to study history in order to inform himself and gain wisdom at the expense of the dead. The time approaches when the life of Anthony offers the young man an instruction more germane than that of Augustus. Émile will scarcely be able to recognise himself clearly in the strange material which his new studies will bring to him, but he will know in advance how to avoid the illusions of passion before they have developed, and, seeing that, in all ages, they have blinded men, he will have prior warning that they may blind him in his turn if he delivers himself up to them. These lessons, I know, are ill suited to him, but remember that they are not the ones I wished him to draw from his study. At the outset I had another object and, surely, if this object is not attained then the teacher is at fault.

[1] *It will be recalled that* Robinson Crusoe *was the only book allowed to Émile in childhood.*

Remember that as soon as selfishness (*l'amour propre*) has developed, the self in relation to others is ceaselessly active, and nothing the young man observes of others is without significance in terms of himself. He constantly compares himself with others.... With regard to my Émile, if it transpires at any time that the parallels he draws lead him to wish himself more to be another than himself, be that other Socrates or Cato, all is lost; he who begins to make himself into a stranger is not far from forgetting himself altogether.

What then makes for a valid study of mankind? A great desire to understand them, a great impartiality of judgment, a heart sensitive enough to comprehend all human passions and yet calm enough not to experience them. If, in life, there is a time favourable to this study it is the one that I have chosen for Émile: earlier than this men would have been as strangers; later he would have been one of them. Opinion (convention), the play of which he now sees, has not yet secured dominion over him; the passions, the effects of which he now understands, do not agitate his heart. He is a man, he interests himself in his brothers; he is equitable, he judges his equals. Now, surely, if he judges aright he will not wish to be in the place of any other, for the object of all the agony of mind they give themselves stems from prejudices he does not have; to him they appear to be but castles in the air. For himself, all that he desires is within his reach. Upon whom must he depend when he is sufficient unto himself and free from prejudice? He has the power of his arms, good health,[1] temperateness, few needs all of which he can satisfy. Brought up in the greatest liberty, the greatest evil he can conceive is servitude. He pities those wretched kings, enslaved to all who obey them; he pities those false wiseacres, chained to their vain reputations; he pities the wealthy fools, martyrs to their displays; he pities the showy voluptuaries whose lives are spent in boredom in order to appear pleasurable.[2] He would pity the enemy who would do him harm, because in that enemy's viciousness he sees misery. He would tell himself, 'In giving way to the need to do harm this man has made his fate dependent upon my own.'

One step more and our goal is attained. Selfish love (*amour propre*) is a valuable instrument but dangerous; frequently it hurts the hand which wields it and it rarely does good without bad. Émile, considering his place among men and finding himself so happily placed, will be tempted to attribute to his own reason the work of yours, and to

[1] *In a footnote Rousseau says that health and strength must be thought of as among the gifts of nature which education has preserved. He does not, however, contend that education consists in strong and healthy growth.*

[2] *One may recall Rousseau's own disillusion with the fashionable world and with those whose cynical attitude caused him (he maintained) to place his children in institutions. (See Introduction, page 5.)*

attribute to his own merit that which he owes to good fortune. He will say to himself, 'I am wise; other men are fools.' He will pity and scorn them whilst the more congratulating himself upon his own worth. This is the error we must most fear because it is the most difficult to eradicate. If he remained in this state he would have gained little from all our care, and if I had to make a choice I do not know that I would not rather the illusions of prejudice than those of arrogance and pride. (I) 290/291/292. (V) 205/206.

The passage reveals something of the nature of the distinction between love of self (*amour de soi*) and selfish love (*amour propre*). It also reveals something of the puzzle which surrounds the distinction. Émile, one must assume by the whole account so far, has been brought up in a manner which should not encourage the latter. Yet Émile will be tempted to the opinions given above. It would seem that *amour-propre* must therefore have at least as solid a foundation in nature as has *amour de soi*. If this were the case, then a reliance upon the beneficence of natural endowment seems to be rather less wise than Rousseau insists that it is.

The puzzle is not resolved in any way by what now follows. In a short paragraph in which Rousseau points out that the truly great man can both realise his stature and retain his modesty, knowing his wisdom is but a gift. The virtue of the good man, however, is of his own making. Rousseau then sets himself to consider what must be done in order to cure the state of mind so bemoaned in the paragraph now under discussion. This would seem to be a tacit admission that nature requires a corrective in certain cases. It can only be presumed that the solution to the puzzle lies in the fact that *amour-propre* is being considered in the context of a corrupt society. If this is the case the paragraph in question is misleading in the extreme, and the notion of education according to nature must undergo a sophistication of a drastic kind in order to accommodate the position now being outlined.

... Let us keep to the common order of things. I have not supposed in my pupil either a transcendent genius or a limited understanding. I chose him from among the ordinary minds in order to show what education could do for men in general.... When, therefore, in consequence of my care, Émile prefers his way of life, his way of seeing things and of caring to that of other men, he reasons aright; but when he believes, as a result of that, that he is of a nature more excellent and happier than others are, he is wrong; he deceives himself; he must be undeceived, or rather the error must be prevented for fear that it becomes too late to exterminate it.

There is no folly of which a man who is not mad cannot be cured save that of vanity; nothing can correct that but experience, if, indeed, it is susceptible to correction at all. At its birth we can, at least, take steps to prevent its growth. Do not, however, waste time in fine reasonings seeking to prove to the adolescent that he is a man as other men are and subject to the same weaknesses. Make him feel it or he will never know it. *Here is another instance which requires an exception to my general rules;*[1] it must be that I expose him deliberately to all the accidents which may prove to him that he is no wiser than we are.... I shall allow flatterers to take every advantage of him; if some giddy fellows drag him into an escapade I shall allow him to run into danger; if he is beguiled by card sharpers into playing with them I shall allow him to become their dupe, let them flatter him, fleece him, strip him, and when, having drained him dry they turn to mock him, I shall even give them my thanks in his presence for the lessons they have been so good as to give him. The only snares from which I shall jealously protect him with all care are those of loose women. The only arrangements I shall make will be to share all the dangers that I allow him to run into and all the affronts I allow him to receive. I will endure all in silence, without complaint or reproach, without saying a single word to him, for, surely, by preserving this discretion most punctiliously, all that he sees me suffer for him will make a greater impression upon his heart than that which he himself suffers.

... If I received a blow whilst discharging my function in respect of Émile, far from avenging myself, I should boast of it; and I doubt if there is in the world a man so vile as not to respect me the more.

It is not the case that the pupil should be allowed to suppose that his master has the same limited insights as his own and the same tendency to allow himself to be beguiled. This opinion is fitting for a child who does not know how to see things, who can compare nothing and who imagines all the world to be at his hand; who gives his confidence only to those who take on this attitude also. But a young man of Émile's age and with his sense is not so foolish as to accept this descent and it would not be good if he did.[2] The confidence he should have in his tutor should be of another sort; it ought to rest upon the authority of reason and on superior understanding, advantages that the young man is able to understand and recognise as valuable to himself. Long experience has convinced the pupil that he is loved by his conductor and guide; that this is a wise person, well informed, who desires his pupil's happiness and knows how to procure it. He ought to know that it is in his best interests to listen to the tutor's advice. (I) 293/294. (V) 207/208.

---

[1] *Editor's italics. The comment confirms the remarks made between these two passages.*

[2] *An interesting warning against making everything too easy for the adolescent which might seem to be somewhat at variance with some current practices.*

One achieves this regard in the pupil, Rousseau continues, by warning him of dangers and consequences. Should he ignore or disbelieve this information, the tutor endures what ensues from that disregard, then, eschewing any recriminations of the 'I told you so' variety, consoles rather than blames him for the results. Thus he wins both his affection ever more strongly and confirms the image of the tutor as wise and far seeing. The moral and ethical overtones of all this are becoming increasingly apparent.

The comment about receiving a blow and of boasting of it rather than seeking to return it reminds one of the Christian principle of turning the other cheek. There is also an implication of Christlike humility in that the tutor does not disdain to share in his pupil's experiences and to bear the consequences of his folly as if he had not the prescience to avoid them. The tutor is no Pharisee it seems. He suffers for his pupil that the pupil may see the light. Now, too, we find, is the time for fables—once more one is reminded of a parallel, that of the telling of parables. As with the parables, the fables are to be taken as complete in themselves and requiring no explanation. If the pupil does not understand the teaching in the fable, then it is of no avail to augment it with explanation. Leave off the moral or maxim at the end. The story should be sufficient for the pupil to discover it for himself. The comment

> The secret of teaching is in making the disciple delight in learning;
> (I) 297. (V) 210.

brings the sudden use of 'disciple', the likeness to such a comment as 'He who has ears, etc.' is once more noteworthy.

However, all this would be somewhat fanciful if it were not for the fact that Rousseau is now but a few pages from his section of the fourth book entitled *Profession De Foi Du Vicaire Savoyard*, wherein he will, as has been mentioned earlier, outline some alternative to the established religious credos which both *Émile* and *Social Contract* offend against. There are one or two more points for him to make before this, however. In the main they are in the nature of the same sort of summing up which has concluded the preceding books of *Émile*.

> ... I believe that if you follow the procedures I have marked out, your pupil will purchase knowledge of mankind and of himself in the best possible market place; that you will have brought him to view

[1] 'Le talent d'instruire est de faire que le disciple se plaise à l'instruction.'

the play of fortune without envying the state of her favourites and to be content as he is without imagining himself wiser than others. You have also begun making him participant in order to make an observer of him; the finishing touches must be effected; for from the pit of the theatre one sees things as they seem to be, upon the boards, one sees them as they are.[1] To take in the whole one must place oneself at a general vantage point; one must come closer to see the details. But what claim can a young man make to enter into the affairs of men? What right has he to be initiated into the mysteries of living? The problems of gaining pleasure are the limited concern of his age; he is responsible only for himself and that is to be as if responsible for nothing. Man is the most paltry of merchandise, and, among our important rights of ownership, that of the self is inferior to all. (I) 298. (V) 211.

The consequence of the last statement is now stated. A corrective follows.

When I see young men at the age of greatest energy and activity limited to purely speculative studies and then, without the least experience, thrown into the world and into the affairs of men, I find it an outrage no less against reason than against nature and am not in the least surprised that so few men know how to conduct themselves.

By what strange turn of mind comes it about that we are taught so many things which are useless whilst the art of doing is counted for nothing? ... You believe you are teaching your children how to live when teaching them certain bodily contortions and certain formulas of speech which signify nothing.

I also believe that I have taught my pupil how to live because I have taught him to live with himself and, more than that, to gain his bread. But this is not enough. To live in the world he must know how to behave with other people; he must know the ways to influence them; he must calculate the action and reaction of individual interests within a society and foresee their outcomes so accurately that he is rarely foiled in his enterprises or will, at least, always adopt the most appropriate means towards success.

... the exercise of social virtues affects the heart deeply with the love of humanity; it is through the doing of good that we are made good; I know of no surer way. Occupy your pupil in all the good deeds which are within his power in order that the interests of the poor are as if his own, that he assists them not only through his purse but with his labours; that he serves and protects them; that he dedicates to them his person and his time; that he acts as their agent: he will not have so noble an employment in his life.

[1] '... du parterre on voit les objets tels qu'ils paraissent, mais de la scène on voit tels qu'ils sont.'

But shall we make of Émile a knight errant, a righter of wrongs, a paladin? ... I do not know.... He will do all that he knows to be useful and good. He will do no more and he knows that nothing is useful and good for him which is unbefitting to his age; he knows that his first duty is to himself; that young men should be mistrustful of themselves and be circumspect in their conduct, respectful in front of their elders, be reticent and discreet when not obliged to speak,[1] modest in things of little importance, but bold and courageous in good works and telling the truth. (I) 298/299/300. (V) 211/212.

The peaceful spirit is an effect of his education, which has never aroused selfish love (amour-propre) or a high opinion of himself, has discouraged him from seeking his pleasures through domination and the sufferings of others. He suffers when he sees suffering; it is a natural sentiment. (I) 301. (V) 213.

Émile loves peace then. Happiness pleases him and when he is able to contribute to it, it is an additional way to share in it. I do not suppose that when he sees unhappiness in people that he will have for them that sterile and cruel pity that is content to be sorry for the misfortunes it is able to cure. His active beneficence provides him with many insights that, had his heart been harder, he would not have acquired or would have been much later gaining. (I) 301. (V) 213.

I do not tire of repeating: formulate all the lessons of young people into actions more than into exposition, that they learn nothing from books which they can learn from experience. (I) 302. (V) 214.

The more I think of it the more I find it true that in putting our good will into action thus, drawing from our success or failure considerations as to the cause, little useful knowledge cannot be cultivated in the mind of a young man, and that, together with what useful knowledge he could gain in a college, he will acquire over and above this a science of still greater importance, which is the application of what is acquired to the purpose of life. (I) 302. (V) 214.

In beginning this work I supposed nothing that could not be observed by anyone as well as myself, for the beginning is the birth of man which all share equally; but the more we advance, I to cultivate nature and you to deprave it, the more we are drawn apart one from the other. My pupil was little different from yours at six years old; for you had not yet had time to distort nature; now they are in no way alike and, at manhood, which approaches, they should show an absolute difference if all my work has not been in vain. They may be more or less equal in the amount that they know but there is no resemblance between the things that they know. You are astonished

[1] This capitalises upon the training in asking only the important questions and not seeking to enslave the attention of others. (See page 93.)

to discover in the one noble sentiments of which the others have not the merest germ; but consider also that the latter are all already philosophers and theologians before Émile even knows what philosophy is and has hardly heard talk of God. (I) 305. (V) 216.

... wishing to form a man according to nature is not to make a savage of him and to send him out into the backwoods. Enclosed within the turmoil of society it is sufficient that he does not allow himself to be carried away either by the passions or the prejudices of men; that he sees with his own eyes; has his own feelings; that he is governed only by the authority of true reason. (I) 306. (V) 217.

I anticipate that many readers will be surprised by my following through my pupil for all this first stage of life without speaking to him of religion. At fifteen years of age he does not know if he has a soul and perhaps, even at eighteen, he is not yet ready to learn of it. If he learns too soon there is risk he will never understand.

The obligation of belief assumes the possibility ... the child who professes Christianity, what does he believe? That which he can conceptualise and this is so little of what he is made to say that if you tell him the opposite he will adopt it willingly. (I) 310. (V) 220.

Rousseau has now come to the point where he must put forward some account of the place of religious belief and religious instruction. He does not wish to follow Diderot into Atheism. He does not wish to follow established practice and baptise children into the Church at any early age. He deplores the notion that the child should be expected to take on the religion of his father. What then?

The solution is very simple it seems to me; we will attach him neither to this creed nor that, but we will seek to put him in a condition to choose that which the best use of his reason directs him.

There is no question then that Émile will have a religion, but there remains the very large question as to just what this religion will be. At this point Rousseau launches into the autobiographical.[1]

I guarantee the facts now to be reported; they actually happened to the author of the paper that I now transcribe. It is for you to see if one can draw from these reflections anything of use for the problem to be solved. I do not put forward the notions of either the author or myself for your rule; I offer them for your examination.

Thirty years ago, in an Italian town, there was a young man, an exile from his own land and reduced to the direst poverty. He was

---

[1] *As has been pointed out in the Introduction, to say that Rousseau becomes autobiographical is by no means to say that he reports with accuracy.*

born a Calvinist but the course of his folly had the consequence that he found himself a fugitive in a strange land, without resources, and he changed his religion for a morsel of bread. There was in the town a hospice for proselytes; he gained admission to it. (I) 314. (V) 223.

There follows a condemnation of the hospice as a place where immorality was rife and where there was a tyrannical rule of a nature as to be all but unsupportable. The young man is in despair. He is rescued by a worthy priest, one who was poor and in need but who helped the young man to escape.

Having escaped from vice to re-enter poverty the young man fought vainly against his fate: at one time he believed he had overcome it. At the first smile of Fortune his misfortunes and his protector were alike forgotten. He was quickly punished for this ingratitude; all his hopes vanished. His youth was to his advantage but his wild ideas ruined all.... Fallen back into his initial distress, without bread, without asylum, prepared to die of hunger, he remembered his benefactor. (I) 315. (V) 224.

The priest once more takes him in and shares his frugal means with him. He himself had preferred poverty and exile rather than a fashionable living where dependence upon patronage constantly forced distortions of a simple faith to accord with the sophistications of behaviour among such people.

A natural affinity with the young fugitive was his and he questioned the young man with care. He saw that ill fortune already blemished his heart, that opprobium and contempt had sapped his courage, and that his pride, transformed into bitter spite, showed him in the injustice and harshness of men nothing but the baseness of their nature and the mockery of the notion of virtue. He had seen that religion was then a mask for self interest and the holy rites a cover for hypocrisy; he had seen, in the subtleties of vain disputes, heaven and hell given as prizes for the play of words; he had seen the sublime and primitive idea of the divine disfigured by the distorted imaginations of men, and, finding that in order to believe in God he must renounce the power of reason received from Him, he held in equal disdain our ridiculous ravings and the object to which they were directed. (I) 315/316. (V) 224/225.

Here is a renewal of the polemic against established custom, this time fully directed upon established religion. Only a flight from all this can rescue the individual from corruption. But not a flight from religious belief:

The neglect of all religion leads to the neglect of all duties of man.

This progress was already more than half accomplished in the heart of the libertine. However, this was not a person born bad,[1] but incredulity and misery were suffocating the natural in him little by little, rapidly dragging him into ruin, fitting him only for the ways of a knave and the morality of the atheist. (I) 316. (V) 225.

I am tired of talking in the third person, it is a superfluous stratagem because you know very well my dear fellow citizen that this wretched fugitive is myself. (I) 317. (V) 225.

Thus unburdened Rousseau now describes the priest's efforts on his behalf. These correspond very closely with the tutor's way with Émile of course. There is little exposition or exhortation and much attendance upon the young Rousseau's questionings. By watching the ways of the priest Rousseau declares that he came to understand that belief in God need not be accompanied by the distortions and hypocrisies described in the passages quoted. Finally, Rousseau comes to the point of asking the priest to inform and correct him in his opinions and confusions, and it is at this point that the priest lays out for him the faith by which he lives. This is the section specially titled *Profession De Foi Du Vicaire Savoyard*. All but immediately it is disclosed that the priest had himself gone 'the way of all flesh' and offended against the sanctity of marriage by an illicit relationship, the more heinous, of course, because to be a priest involved a vow of celibacy. All this had come about because the haste to get him into the Church, allied with his desire to please his parents, had occasioned him to promise what he did not understand and could not fulfil.

The priest now recounts to the young man his struggles with himself. Abandoning all creeds can man, in reason, come to a conclusion that there is no God? In other words, given man in a state of nature, man as himself, uninfluenced by already extant dogmas, is it the case that he would or could apprehend and come to believe in the idea of a God?

The argument is a long and complicated one which both recapitulates much that has gone before and continues to lay foundations for the book that is to accompany *Émile*. There is approximately a quarter of the total length of the fourth book yet to be read at this point. The creed takes up about half of that before Rousseau resumes his account of Émile in the shape of a general and lengthy summing

---

[1] *This is, of course, to make explicit the case against the doctrine of Original Sin which underlies much of what has been quoted here. Not born bad but made bad is the message.*

up. It is plainly impossible to lay out much more in a work of this length. Perhaps the essential contention is as follows:

> I believe therefore that the world is governed by a will that is powerful and wise; I see it, or rather I feel it, and it is of great importance to me to know this. But this same world; is it everlasting or has it been created? Is there a single source of all things? Are there two or many? And what is their nature? I do not know.

> ... Whether matter is eternal or created, or that its origin is passive or not, it is forever certain that all is one and speaks of one unique intelligence, for I see nothing that is not ordered within a single system and which does not contribute to the same end, the preservation of everything within that established order. This being who wills and is able to work his will, this being of complete self sufficiency, who, in a word and whoever he is, moves the universe and orders all things, I call God. (I) 335. (V) 239.

We now have Rousseau's adumbration of the author of Nature, and the basis to the argument that Nature moves about us and within us to a pattern upon which we cannot improve.

It is a unifying belief in a unifying Deity. It is therefore the case that man may come to know of him independently of specific creeds; a natural man's natural religion as it were.[1] On the other hand, any creed which a man may hold (the priest is a Catholic) does not impede him from this acquaintance and from the guidance and succour of God. What Rousseau is arguing is that religion, as everything else, can be according to nature or contrary to it.

It is now time to turn to a brief consideration of the final book of *Émile*. The young man, now entered upon the world, will want a wife. The wife will become a mother. At the outset of *Émile* Rousseau had much to say about the shortcomings of mothers as he found them. For the new man, in the perfection of an education according to nature, there must be a new woman, no less perfect as a woman than Émile as a man.

[1] *See* Philosophy of the Enlightenment, *by E. Cassirer, for an interesting account of the notion of natural religion.*

Chapter Five

MAN AND WOMAN

<hr>

We have come to the last act of the play of youth; but we have yet to reveal the denouement.

It is not good that man should be alone. Émile is a man; we have promised him a companion and we must give him one. That companion is Sophy.

Sophy ought to be truly a woman as Émile is truly a man, that is to say that she should have all the attributes of her species and her sex which enable her to fill her place in the physical and moral order. (I) 445. (V) 321.

Thus Rousseau begins the final book of *Émile*. What follows has frequently been criticised as a denigration of women, as a statement of male superiority and as a radical underestimation of the possibilities of women in terms of intellectual capacity. The reader must have recourse to the original to decide this for himself. Certainly it would seem fair to say that Rousseau's account would be unacceptable in the twentieth century in a great many details and that much of his theorising is baseless in fact. On the other hand, it must be born in mind that he was NOT writing in the twentieth century and that it may well be the case that his view of women, as expressed in this book, is a more liberal one than might generally have been found at the time when it was written. It might even be said that something of the frank recognition that men and women are different in important ways which are not merely anatomical might profitably be restated in the present to counteract some of the more extreme pleadings for 'equality'. One would not want to draw the same conclusions from the existence of these differences as are drawn by Rousseau in respect of what constitutes an appropriate education for a girl in distinction from a boy, nor to assign the same role to woman in society as Rousseau does.

In view of the above, it would be pointless to draw upon this last part of *Émile* to anything like the extent that has been done in respect of preceding sections. Much of what it contains could only be paraded as an historical curiosity. The following passages will serve to give some indication of the general tenor of the account as well as to highlight certain interesting positions which might be said to have a less limited value.

In all that is not a characteristic of sex, woman is as a man: she has the same organs, the same needs, the same faculties.... In all concerning sex men and women are in everything relative to each other and in everything different; the difficulty for comparison of the one with the other is that of determining what is attributable to sex and what is not.... Seen from these two points of view we find so many resemblances and so many dissimilarities between them that it is perhaps one of the marvels of nature that she has made two beings both so similar and so different. These resemblances and these differences are bound to exert their influence upon the moral; this consequence is plain to see, consistent with experience, and shows the futility of disputes over the superiority or the equality of the sexes: as if each sex, moving within its pattern towards its particular destiny as marked out by nature, were not more perfect in conforming to itself than to the other!

In the union of the sexes each contributes to the common end but not in the same manner. From this diversity arises the first assignable difference between the moral relations of the one with the other. The one should be active and strong, the other passive and weak: it is necessary that the one have the will and the power; it is sufficient for the other to offer little resistance.[1] This principle established it ensues that the woman is made especially to please the man. If man ought to be pleasing to her in his turn the necessity is less direct: his merit is in his power; he pleases by the very fact that he is strong. I concede that we have not here the law of love, but it is that of nature which is prior to that of love itself. (I) 445/446. (V) 321/322.

The act of loving has consequences so different for the two sexes. Is it therefore natural that they should both display the same boldness in entrusting themselves to it?

... (in) a hot country where more women than men are born and tyrannise the men, the latter would become their victims and be dragged to their death with never a chance of defending themselves. (I) 447. (V) 322.

[1] *All other considerations aside it is a matter of some doubt as to what is here put forward could validly be described as to do with morals.*

That is if the men were not the stronger sex.

Whether the female shares the passion of the man or not and wishes, or not, to satisfy it, she always repulses and resists, but not always with the same resolution and with the same success. For the attack to be successful the attacked must permit or direct it ...

Thus we find a third consequence of the constitution of the sexes; the stronger is the master in appearance yet is, in fact, dependent upon the weaker ... by an invariable law of nature. (I) 447. (V) 322.

See how we are led unconsciously from the physical to the moral and how from the grosser union of the sexes arises, little by little, the gentle laws of love. The sway of woman is not stemmed from the wish of man but because nature so decrees it.... Women, you say, are not perpetually carrying children. No; but their proper function is in doing so.... If, here and there, there are women who bear few children, what of that? The woman's state is no less that of being a mother and is it not the case that the general laws of nature and morals provide for this state? (I) 449. (V) 324.

Immediately it is shown that men and women are not nor ought to be of the same constitution, character and temperament, it follows that they ought not to have the same education.... Does it follow that they (women) ought to be brought up in ignorance of everything, limited solely to housework? Is the man to have a servant or a companion? Will he deprive himself of her greatest charm; her society? ... Undoubtedly not; this is not what nature decrees, who gives to women so agreeable and subtle a mind; on the contrary, nature wishes them to think, to consider, to love, to have understanding, to cultivate their minds as they care for their figures.... They should learn many things but only those things which are suitable. (I) 453. (V) 326.

... the entire education of women ought to be in relation to man. To please him, to be of use to him, to love and honour him, to rear his children, to tend him in manhood, counsel him, console him, make life pleasant and sweet for him; these are the duties of woman in all ages and what they should learn in their infancy. (I) 455. (V) 328.

It is certain that little girls wish with all their hearts to know how to adorn their dolls.... Here we have a clue as to the first lessons we will give her: they are not tasks put upon her but favours bestowed. It is a fact that the great majority of little girls learn to read and to write with repugnance, but as for taking to a needle, that they learn with the greatest willingness.... Once this route is opened it is easy to follow; dress making, embroidery and lace working arise of themselves....

This voluntary progress extends itself with ease into drawing and design because this art is not unconnected to those in which so much pleasure is taken, but I would not wish it to be applied to landscape and still less to figures.... In general, if it is important to limit the studies of a male to that which is useful, it is yet more important in respect of the female ... if I would not have a young boy pressed to learn to read, I have even more reason for wishing that young girls should not before they clearly see the value of it.... After all, why is it necessary to the happiness of a girl that she should read and write? Has she a house to manage? Many of them make more abuse than use of this fatal knowledge; and all are much too curious for them not to learn it without force when they have the choice and the occasion. Perhaps they should learn to calculate before all.... If the little girl cannot obtain cherries for her lunch except by doing some arithmetic I can only say that she will soon learn. (I) 459/460. (V) 331.

Do not take from them gaiety, laughter, noise and lively games; but guard against their tiring of one and running to another; do not allow a single moment in their lives when they go uncurbed. Accustom them to discontinuing their games and returning to their other cares without a murmur. Habit alone needs to be established in this, for nature first decrees it. The result of this constraining habit is a docility of which woman stands in need all her life, since she will always be subordinate to a man or to the judgments of men and never allowed to elevate her judgments above his. The first and most important quality for a woman is that of meekness; made to obey a creature so imperfect as a man, so often so full of vices, she ought to learn early on to endure the injustice and the wrongdoings of her husband without complaint; it is not for him that she should but for herself. Sourness and headstrong behaviour in a woman do nothing but increase her misfortunes and the misdeeds of the husbands who feel that it is not with these weapons that they will be vanquished.... Each should preserve the tone of his or her sex; too gentle a husband makes for a nagging wife, but, given the man is not a monster, the sweetness of a woman will reclaim and triumph over him sooner or later. (I) 463. (V) 333/334.

One ought not to repress the babble of a young girl in the way one did with a young boy, by the stark question 'What is the good of that?' but by this other question which it is no easier to answer, 'What effect will that have?' ... If one ought not to permit young boys to ask indiscreet questions there is the greater reason why they should be forbidden to little girls for if their curiosity is satisfied or clumsily evaded the consequence is greater; so eager are they to uncover the mysteries hidden from them and so adept at discovering them. (I) 471. (V) 339.

Rousseau's model of a 'natural woman' in distinction to a 'natural man' harks back to a work earlier than *Émile* but which contains presages of *The Social Contract* in the same way as does *Émile*. This work is the novel *Julie ou la Nouvelle Heloise*.[1] Like *Émile*, it has considerable length. It has considerably more of Rousseau himself within it than has *Émile*.

From the passages quoted from the final book of *Émile* it is plain that the education of women is proscriptive in the very way to be deplored in respect of Émile himself. Sophy should never be without a curb. She must always be brought to consider the effect of what she says and does upon other people. She must grow to accommodate and to placate the possible vagaries of her husband and so guide him with tact and subtlety into ways of thought and action which are commendable. In this way she does not falsify her nature as a woman and assists man to move both himself and his society towards a state nearer to accordance with nature. Even when mankind is not within a state of nature but enmeshed within the toils and customs of a society which desperately requires reformation, woman must match and subordinate her own feelings to the best interests of that society, by which is meant those characteristics in it which would remain even when the desired reformation took place. Among these characteristics would be the institution of marriage. Should it be, therefore, that a woman's love for a man could, for whatever reason, result in no socially beneficial contractual relationship then that love must remain unfulfilled. This is in the interests of a model society; interests that will, in fact, emerge as the woman's also, for all that, the course followed is a painful and difficult one.

Rousseau's novel has a plot which depicts all this. Julie, the heroine, turns from her lover, one Saint-Preux, to devote herself to the man her family see as suitable for her to marry. In a society which served man as he developed according to nature this man must have been Saint-Preux himself of course, but society is not thus. As a consequence, Julie must sacrifice her love for Saint-Preux, since to do otherwise would be to sully and distort it. In doing this she preserves love; she does not repudiate it.

Plainly there is something very odd about this. Rousseau is bending his view of the prime value of man as himself to the social and political thesis that will be the *Social Contract*. He is also distorting his characters in curious ways, so doing no service to his work when it is evaluated as literature. Finally, it is difficult to see how Rousseau can escape the charge that he is falsifying his own thesis by allowing social convention to subvert a deep and abiding relationship between two people which is of a nature demanding of a

[1] See *Introduction, page 11.*

certain consummation. In an attempt to evade the charge, one might suggest, lies the reason for the length of the novel. It is true that novels were long at this time, but this seems insufficient as an explanation.

Within the compass of this book it would not be possible to give a sufficiency of quotations to present a coherent picture of all this. The following may give some small indication.

From a description of the first engraving illustrating the book

Julie (is) fair of complexion, gentle of countenance, tender, modest, and altogether charming. She has natural grace without the least affectation; an elegant simplicity ... few ornaments. ...

From the Preface

I have seen the morals of my time and I have published these letters. Oh that I had lived in a time when I should have consigned them to the fire! ... This book is not at all for popular circulation and will suit few readers ... all the sentiments lie beyond the scope of those who do not believe in virtue. It will be deplored by the sanctimonious, the libertines, the philosophers; it will shock the courtesans and scandalise the honest women.

From a note by Julie

Do not have the idea that your removal is necessary. A virtuous heart is capable of controlling the passions, of remaining silent. ...

Letter iv de (from) Julie

I have neglected nothing to arrest the progress of this disastrous passion (but) everything foments the ardour that possesses me—all my efforts are vain and I love you in spite of myself.

From a letter to Julie from her cousin

... I have not a moment of repose whilst away from you, for if you fear danger it cannot be entirely without foundation. It is true that safety is easily secured: two words to your mother and all is finished, but I understand you: you do not wish for an expedient which finishes everything: you wish greatly to rid yourself of the possibility of succumbing but not of the honour of striving against the possibility. Oh poor cousin! ... The baron d'Etrange consenting to give his daughter, his only child, to a commoner without fortune! Is it to be hoped for?

From a letter by Julie which appears towards the conclusion of the book

In this she urges the man who loves her, but could not marry her because he was 'a commoner without fortune', to marry Claire, her cousin, and so find the socially sanctified happiness she had herself known in her own marriage. This counsel does not imply a denial of Julie's love for Saint-Preux—only a way of loving that does not infringe the socially desirable state of marriage, without which it is not possible to love in actuality and be blameless.

> ... It is necessary to renounce our schemes. All is changed, my dear friend; let us endure this without complaint for it comes from the hand of one wiser than we are. We dreamed of being reunited but this was not good. It is a kindness of heaven which has prevented it; doubtless heaven does prevent unhappiness.
>
> ... My friend, I leave at the right time[1] for both of us; I have done this with joy and this is in no way a cruel departure. After so much sacrifice I count as little the only thing left for me to do....
>
> Think that there remains for you another Julie and do not forget what you owe to her. Each of you loses half of your life, unite therefore in order to preserve the other ... Claire and Julie should be so thoroughly identified that it will not be possible to separate them in your affection....
>
> Could my soul exist without you? Without you what happiness could I taste? No; I do not leave you. I am going to wait for you. Virtue, which separated us on earth will unite us in eternity. I die with this sweet anticipation; only too happy to give my life as payment for the right to love you always without crime and to tell you it one more time.

If some of Rousseau's notions as to the nature of women appear somewhat curious when we read them in the last book of *Émile* we may now, at least, observe that they take their rise from his thinking as it is expressed in this novel. Ironically enough they seem to stem less from his own experience than from the necessity to bend that experience to suit a social thesis. Once again we come upon paradox. How can one reconcile the underlying thesis to this novel with such a statement as one reads in the second book of *Émile*?

Human institutions are one mass of folly and contradiction.

---

[1] *Julie had rescued one of her children from drowning and so contracted an illness.*

Chapter Six

FROM DU CONTRAT SOCIAL

I wish to discover whether, taking men as they are, and the laws as they are able to be, it is possible to establish some justifiable and sure administration of society.

Man is born free, and everywhere he is in chains. Those who believe themselves the masters of others are no less enslaved than those they rule. How does this happen? I do not know. What makes it justifiable? I believe I may be able to answer that question. (II) 39/41. (VII) 5.

... the social order is a sacred right which serves for a basis to all others. However this right does not come from nature; it is therefore founded on conventions. One must ask what these conventions are.

The oldest of all societies and the single natural one is that of the family. Yet the children remain bound to the father only so long as they need his protection.... If they continue to remain united it is no longer a natural tie but a voluntary association, and the family itself is maintained only by a convention.

This common liberty is a consequence of the nature of man. (II) 41/42. (VII) 6.

The family is, therefore, so it would seem, the first model for political societies ... (all members) are born equal and free (and) only alienate their liberty to gain that which is of usefulness. (II) 42. (VII) 6.

The strongest are never strong enough to be always master if they do not transform force into right and obedience into duty.

To renounce liberty is to renounce the quality of man and the rights of humanity together with its duties. Such a renunciation is never satisfied however great the harm it wards off. A renunciation such as this is incompatible with the nature of man; when once he is deprived of free will his actions are deprived of all morality. (II) 44. (VII) 8.

I will suppose that men have arrived at that point where the obstacles in their path preventing their preservation when in a state of nature remove from the power of each individual the ability to maintain himself in that state. (II) 50. (VII) 14.

Now as men are unable to engender new powers within themselves but merely to unify and direct those which exist, they have no other choice in preserving themselves than to form, by aggregation, a sum of forces sufficient to overcome the obstacles ... to act in concert. (II) 50. (VII) 14.

If ... we exclude from the social contract that which is not essential, we shall find it reduces to the terms which follow:

> Each of us places in common his person and his power under the supreme direction of the general will; and we receive, as a body, each member as an indivisible part of the whole.

It can be seen by this formula that the act of association comprises a reciprocal engagement between the public and the individual, and that each individual, contracting, so to speak, with himself, finds himself engaged under a dual relationship; namely as a member of the Sovereign dealing with individuals, and as a member of the society dealing with the Sovereign. (II) 51/52. (VII) 15/16.

Now the Sovereign being formed only of the individuals who compose it, neither has nor is able to have any interest contrary to theirs; with the consequence that the sovereign power has no need to issue guarantees to its subjects because it is impossible that the body should wish to harm all its members, and we shall see hereafter that neither is it able to do harm to any one particular. (II) 54. (VII) 17.

... each individual is able as a man to have a private will contrary or dissimilar to the general will which is his as a citizen (member of the Sovereign) ... he may want to enjoy the rights of a citizen without wishing to fulfil the duties of a subject; an injustice which would cause the ruin of the body politic. (II) 54. (VII) 18.

From the last statement it is argued that such a man is acting against himself and his own freedom and would not therefore will other than that he be prevented from this.

It follows from what has preceded that the general will is always right and tends always to the advantage of the whole.... (II) 66. (VII) 26.

It is the case that there is often considerable difference between the will of all (the sum of private wills) and the general will (which regards only the common interest) ... but remove from the will of all the pluses and minuses which discount each other, and the sum of the differences remain as the general will. (II) 66. (VII) 26.

Every citizen should speak his opinion only from himself. (II) 67. (VII) 27.

The general will is always right but the judgments that guide it are not always clear. It is necessary to make people see things as they are, sometimes as they ought to be, to show them the right road which they seek, guarding them against the seductions of the private will, relating, in their eyes, time and place, to balance the lure of present and sensible advantage against the danger of distant and hidden disasters.

From this is born the necessity for a legislator. (II) 76. (VII) 35.

And parallel to this argument the necessity for a tutor for Émile.

BIBLIOGRAPHY

(I) Jean-Jacques Rousseau, *Émile ou de l'éducation.*
*Introduction, bibliographie, notes et index analytique
par François et Pierre Richard.* Editions Garnier Frères,
1964

(II) Jean-Jacques Rousseau, *Du Contrat Social
Chronologie et introduction par Pierre Burgelin.*
Garnier Flammarion, 1966

(III) Jean-Jacques Rousseau, *Les Confessions
Edition intégrale par A. van Bever.* Paris Cres., 1913

(IV) Jean-Jacques Rousseau, *Julie ou la Nouvelle Héloïse
Edition de René Pomeau.* Editions Garnier Frères, 1960

(V) Jean-Jacques Rousseau, *Émile*
Translated by Barbara Foxley: introduction Andre
Boutet De Monvel. Everyman's Library No. 158, Dent

(VI) *Rousseau: The Social Contracte or Principles of Political
Right*
Translated with an historical and critical introduction
and notes by Henry J. Tozer. Social Science Series, Allen
& Unwin, 1948

(VII) *The Social Contract by Jean-Jacques Rousseau*
An eighteenth-century translation completed, revised,
edited, with an introduction by Charles Frankel. Hafner
Publishing Co. N.Y. (12th printing), 1964

(VIII) Jean-Jacques Rousseau, *The Confessions*
Translated Cohen. Penguin Classics.

(IX) Broome, J. H., *Rousseau: A Study of his Thought.* Arnold,
1963

(X) Green, F. C., *J. J. Rousseau: A critical study of his life and
writings.* Cambridge University Press, 1955

(XI) McDonald, J., *Rousseau and the French Revolution.* Athlone
Press, 1965

(XII) Ed. F. Watkins, *Rousseau: Political Writings.* Nelson, 1953

(XIII) Cassirer, E., *The Philosophy of the Enlightenment.* Beacon
Press, Boston, 1955

Educational Thinkers Series

This series aims to meet the widely-felt need for *modern* editions
of the writings of major educational philosophers. Each volume
contains carefully chosen selections representing the principal
writings of a philosopher, together with a substantial Introduction.
Students ask why they should study thinkers of the past:
these volumes endeavour to answer that question by establishing
the philosopher's relevance to our own times. The editing, and
the Introduction, show the philosopher's links both with the
received ideas of his period and with present-day problems
in education. Each volume places the thinker in his historical
setting, and points out the propagandist purpose which may often
be found in the educational philosopher's writings.
The works of foreign philosophers will generally be newly
translated for the series.
Development of the series is guided by Dr. Leslie Perry, Senior
Lecturer in Philosophy at London University Institute of
Education. Editors of the individual volumes are selected for
their scholastic ability in the philosophy of education and their
knowledge of particular philosophers, coupled with appropriate
linguistic ability.

Matthew Arnold edited by James Gribble
Bertrand Russell, A. S. Neill,
Homer Lane, W. H. Kilpatrick:
Four progressive educators edited by Leslie R. Perry
Aristotle edited by George Howie
Herbert Spencer edited by Ann Low-Beer
Other volumes in preparation

97258